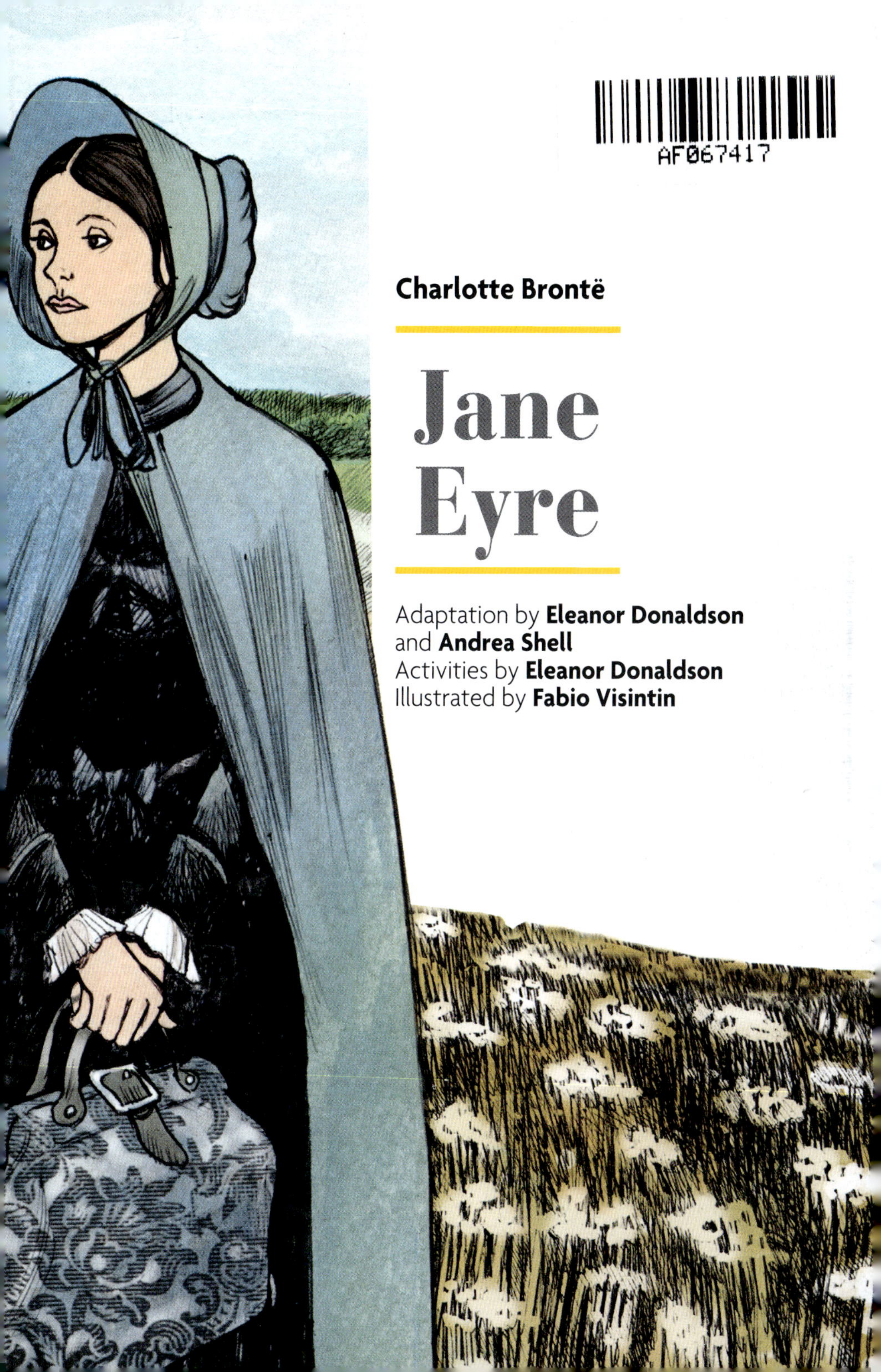

Charlotte Brontë

Jane Eyre

Adaptation by **Eleanor Donaldson** and **Andrea Shell**
Activities by **Eleanor Donaldson**
Illustrated by **Fabio Visintin**

The design, production and distribution of educational materials for the CIDEB brand are managed in compliance with the rules of Quality Management System which fulfils the requirements of the standard ISO 9001 (Rina Cert. No. 24298/02/S - IQNet Reg. No. IT-80096)

Content editor: Maria Grazia Donati
Editor: Nicoletta Baldini
for Equilibri servizi editoriali
Design: Sara Fabbri, Erika Barabino
Page layout: Annalisa Possenti
Picture research: Alice Graziotin

Art Director: Nadia Maestri

© 2018 Black Cat
First edition: March 2018

DEALINK, DEAFLIX are trademarks licensed by De Agostini SpA

Picture credits:
Shutterstock; iStockphoto; De Agostini Picture Library: 4; National Portrait Gallery, London, UK/Photo © Brian Seed/Bridgeman Images: 5; © Look and Learn/Bridgeman Images: 67; The Stapleton Collection/Bridgeman Images: 69; Webphoto: 70; BBC FILMS/Album/MONDADORI PORTFOLIO: 76; MSP Travel Images/Alamy Stock Photo: 98l; iSpice/Alamy Stock Photo: rb; Bridgeman Images: 99; The Bowes Museum, Barnard Castle, County Durham, UK/Bridgeman Images: 101r.

All rights reserved. No part of this book may be reproduced, stored in a retrieval system or transmitted, in any form or by any means, electronic, mechanical, photocopying, recording or otherwise, without the written permission of the publisher.

We would be happy to give you further information concerning our material and receive your comments.

info@blackcat-cideb.com
blackcat-cideb.com

Printed in Italy, by Litoprint s.r.l., Genoa

Contents

4	▶	**The life of Charlotte Brontë**
8	▶	**Before you read**
11	▶	**Chapter 1**
		The red room
		Chapter 2
		School days — 17
		Chapter 3
		Life as a governess — 22
		Chapter 4
		The incident in the attic — 29
		Chapter 5
		Surprising news — 35
		Chapter 6
		A secret and a marriage — 41
		Chapter 7
		A new life — 47
		Chapter 8
		An unexpected proposal — 52
		Chapter 9
		Mr Rochester — 60
67	▶	**Dossier**
		The woman in the attic — 67
		Locations in *Jane Eyre* — 72
		Cinema — 76
77	▶	**Activities**

`n.track` 🔊 THE STORY IS FULLY RECORDED

The life of Charlotte Brontë

Charlotte Brontë was born in Thornton, Yorkshire, in the north of England in 1816. She was the third daughter of Patrick Brontë, a clergyman,[1] and of Maria Branwell. The family moved to Haworth Parsonage[2] in North Yorkshire in 1800. The couple had five daughters and one son. When Charlotte's mother died in 1821, the children's aunt, Elizabeth Branwell, went to live with the family. The children only had each other for company. They all loved reading and they created a magical world of their own, based on the stories that they read. As a starting point they took the brother Branwell's toy soldiers, and they invented their own fantasy lands, called Angria and Gondal. They wrote histories and newspapers for these imaginary countries. In 1824, the four eldest girls were sent to a boarding school[3] at Cowan Bridge, which Charlotte later used as a model for Lowood School in *Jane Eyre*. The severe conditions at the school were partly responsible for the deaths of Charlotte's sisters, Elizabeth and Maria, who both died in the same year, 1825.

---

1. **clergyman**: priest.
2. **parsonage**: house where the priest and his family live.
3. **boarding school**: school in which the pupils live during the school term.

Charlotte herself was never completely healthy after her difficult time as a pupil at the school.

Charlotte was much happier at her second school, Roe Head. There she made one or two friends, who appeared in her novels in various forms. She later returned to the school as a teacher. She was, for a short time, governess[4] to two families, and then opened her own school at Haworth with her sister Emily (author of *Wuthering Heights*, published in 1847).

In 1842 Charlotte and Emily went to study languages at a school in Brussels, called the Pensionnat Heger. During her stay, Charlotte fell deeply in love with Monsieur Heger, the director. He didn't return her love, and never replied to the letters that she sent him after she returned to Haworth. Charlotte later used this experience in her novel *Villette* (published in 1853).

Charlotte's first novel, *The Professor*, was not accepted by the publisher, but she then wrote *Jane Eyre*, which was a great success,

---

4. governess : woman who taught small children privately.

▶ The Brontë sisters (about 1834) by their brother Patrick Branwell Brontë. From the left: Anne, Emily and Charlotte.

and for which she is very famous. Both Charlotte and her sisters, Anne and Emily, published their work under male pseudonyms,[5] as people did not respect women writers at that time. When the public realised that *Jane Eyre* was written by a woman, some critics accused Jane of being coarse[6] and unfeminine.[7] Charlotte Brontë's family life was not happy. Her beloved sisters, Anne and Emily, both died while still young and her brother, Patrick, died of alcoholism after living an insignificant life. In 1854 she agreed to marry her father's curate,[8] Mr Nicholls, but the marriage was short-lived: Charlotte Brontë died in March 1855, at the age of thirty-nine, of an illness connected with childbirth.

Jane Eyre intrigues and gives pleasure to modern readers as much as it did when it was first published in 1847.

1 Comprehension Check • Use the clues to write questions in the correct order about Charlotte Brontë's life using the past tense. Answer the questions. There is an example at the beginning (0).

0. where/born/Charlotte
Q: *Where was Charlotte Brontë born?* A: *In Thornton, in Yorkshire.*
1. many/brothers and sisters/how/have
2. Charlotte/happy/boarding school/at
3. jobs/Charlotte/do
4. Pensionnat Heger/happen/what/at
5. famous/which/novel/for/most
6. why/pseudonyms/use/male/Charlotte/her sisters
7. who/1854/marry
8. old/Charlotte/when/die/how

---

5. pseudonyms : names which writers use instead of their real names.
6. coarse : vulgar, unrefined.
7. unfeminine : with qualities not typical of women.
8. curate : assistant to the priest.

2 Read the text and complete Charlotte's family tree.

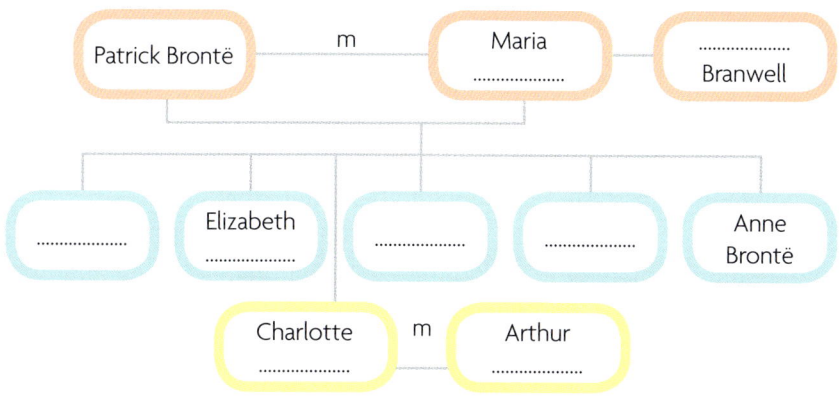

3 Vocabulary • Which of these adjectives can be used to describe Charlotte?

inventive   healthy   passionate   famous   lucky   intelligent

4 Vocabulary • Choose adjectives from the word box to complete the sentences.

healthy   famous   inventive   intelligent   lucky   passionate

1. Charlotte and Emily were .... authors.
2. All of the children were .... They created imaginary worlds.
3. Charlotte was never completely .... after her time at Cowan Bridge school.
4. The Brontë sisters studied hard and were very ....
5. Some people thought that the Brontë's female characters were too ....
6. Charlotte was not .... in love, but she did eventually marry.

5 Writing • Imagine you are Charlotte looking back at your life. Write sentences using the examples to help you talk about the good memories and the bad memories.

I was so happy when I used to .... with my brothers and sisters.
I remember how I happy/excited I felt when ....
I remember how sad/lonely/upset I felt when ....

BEFORE YOU READ

1 Match the words. Choose the right description for the photographs.

a modern   **b** cosy   **c** country   **1** ☐ estate   **2** ☐ flat   **3** ☐ cottage

A ☐   B ☐   C ☐

2 Which of these places would you prefer to live in? Why?

3 The words in the box describe people and places in a 19th century country house and estate. Put the words in the best vocabulary category. Add as many new words as you can in 10 minutes to each category. Compare your new words with another student. Use a dictionary if necessary.

majestic   luxurious   ladies   maid   bedroom   lords   library
servants   chapel   clergyman   enchanting   attic   wealthy
drawing room   elegant   master   housekeeper   beautiful   gardens

Places	People	Descriptions
Library	*Servants*	*Beautiful*

4 Look at the places in the word box (a-f). These are places where Jane lives in the story. Can you guess where the events in 1-6 happen? Return to this page and check your answers at the end of the story.

a Aunt Reed's House   b Lowood School   c Thornfield Hall
d The Rivers' family home   e Jane's cottage   f Ferndean

1. ☐ Jane teaches at the village school and spends her time painting here.
2. ☐ Mr Rochester, Jane's master, moves to a smaller, quieter house.
3. ☐ Jane is a governess in a big house and meets a man who will change her life.
4. ☐ Jane is treated cruelly by her aunt and cousins.
5. ☐ The conditions here are terrible and some children die.
6. ☐ Jane is looked after by kind strangers who become her family.

5 Unscramble the letters to make words to match the description. Exercise 4 has some clues.

1. ropnha – a child that has no parents ....
2. daotp – to become a child's parent by law (if they have no parents, for example) ....
3. cnule – your father or mother's brother ....
4. usocnis – the children of your father or mother's brother or sister ....
5. eiwf – a married woman ....
6. ogevrsnes – a lady who looks after children and teaches them at home ....

6 In *Jane Eyre*, Jane is an orphan. She is looked after (or adopted) by: her uncle/aunt, a maid, a teacher and even strangers. She also looks after other people, for example, as a governess. Answer the questions about family and looking after people.

1. Would you look after someone who was not a family member?
2. Would you like to go to boarding school or be looked after by a governess?
3. Find the word 'role model'. Can you think of any 'role models' in your life?
4. Do you think families today are different to families in the 1800s? Explain your answer.

The Characters

CHAPTER 1

The red room

I do not remember much of my early life. My parents died before I could remember anything about them. I was adopted[1] by my Uncle Reed. The servants tell me that he was a kind man.

He took pity[2] on me. When he was ill and dying, he asked his wife, Mrs Reed, to take care of me as one of her own children. Although she wished to please him, she could not keep her promise.

My name is Jane Eyre and my story really begins when I was 10 years old. I was living in a large, beautiful house but I was not happy. The only person to show me any friendship was the youngest servant, Bessie. I liked the stories she told me when I went to bed. Sometimes she was angry with me, but it was never for long.

---

1. adopt : took (her) into (his) home and became a parent.
2. take pity : to feel sympathy.

CHAPTER 1

My three cousins Eliza, John and Georgiana were older than me. They teased[3] me and never wanted to play with me. If I told Aunt Reed about it, she didn't believe me and she took their side. Sometimes they were very cruel and I was even afraid of them.

Most of all, I was afraid of John Reed. He liked to frighten me and he made me very unhappy.

I often hid from him in a small room. There was a library there and I used to like looking at the pictures in the big books.

One day I was reading a book. I felt happy and safe in my little room, because I knew that John and his sisters were with their mother. But then John got bored and decided to look for me.

'Where's Jane Eyre?' he shouted. I kept very quiet and hoped he would not find me, as he was not a clever boy. But his sister Eliza soon found where I was hiding.

'Here she is,' she called, and I had to come out. I put the book down. John grinned[4] unpleasantly when he saw me.

'What do you want?' I asked him.

He made me stand in front of him. He stared[5] at me for a long time, and then, suddenly, he hit me. 'Now go and stand by the door,' he said.

Now I was really frightened. I knew that John was going to hurt me.

I went and stood near the door.

---

3. tease : laugh and say unkind things.
4. grin : smile.
5. stare : look for a long time.

CHAPTER 1

'I'll teach you to take our property,' said John Reed, and he picked up a large, heavy book from the library and threw it at me.

I tried to get out of the way, but I was too late. It hit me on the head, and I fell.

'You wicked,[6] cruel boy,' I shouted. 'Why do you want to hurt me?' I touched my head. There was blood on it. 'Look what you have done!' I cried.

My words just made John Reed angrier. He ran across the room towards me, and began to hit me again and again. I was very frightened, so I hit him back.

I don't know what I did to John Reed, but it hurt him. He started to call for his mother.

'Mother! Mother!'

Mrs Reed heard the noise and hurried into the room. She didn't seem to see the blood which ran down my face.

'Jane Eyre, you are a bad girl!' she cried. 'Why are you hitting poor John, who is always so good to you?'

No one listened when I tried to say what John had done to me.

Mrs Reed told two of the older servants to take me away.

'Take her to the red room and lock the door,' she told them.

The red room was cold and dark. It had a big bed with heavy curtains and a red carpet.

The curtains were closed. Bessie had told me that Mrs Reed's husband had died in that room. Nobody ever went there at night.

I was very frightened. I cried for help, but nobody came.

'Please help me!' I shouted. 'Don't leave me here alone!'

Still nobody came. I cried for a long time. I was more terrified with every minute that went by.

---

6. wicked : very bad.

I thought I saw shadows near the bed. Then everything suddenly went black, and I think that I fainted. I remembered nothing after that.

When I woke up, I was in my own bed. My head was hurting. Bessie was there with another servant. She asked if I wanted anything to eat or drink.

The doctor was sitting beside the bed. I felt very glad[7] that someone who was not part of the Reed family was in the room with me. 'What happened to me?' I asked him.

'You are ill, Jane,' the doctor answered. 'Bessie says that you have cried a lot. Why did you cry so much?'

'I cry because I am miserable,' I replied.

The doctor looked puzzled.[8] 'What made her ill yesterday?' he asked the other servant.

'She fell, sir,' was the reply. I could not waste this opportunity. I wanted the doctor to know the truth about my life with Mrs Reed and my cousins. 'I was knocked down,' I said. 'But that did not make me ill. I was shut up in a dark, cold room until after dark.'[9]

---

7. **glad :** very happy
8. **puzzled :** confused, unable to understand.
9. **after dark :** night time.

CHAPTER 1

The doctor sent Bessie and the servant away, and then he asked me, 'Are you unhappy here with your aunt and cousins?'

'Yes, I am,' I told him. 'I'm very unhappy.'

The doctor looked at me kindly. 'I see,' he said. 'Would you like to go away to school?'

'Oh yes, I think that I would,' I answered.

The doctor looked at me again for a long time, and then went downstairs to speak to Mrs Reed.

Much later, Mrs Reed came to see me and told me that she had decided to send me to school.

A few days later, I left my aunt's house to go to school. I knew that Mrs Reed and my cousins were glad to see me leave. They did not want me to go back for holidays. I had lived with them for as long as I could remember, but I was not really sad to leave. Even the servants treated me badly. The only person I would miss was Bessie.

'Perhaps I'll be happy at school,' I thought. 'Maybe there will be someone who likes me. I could find some friends there.'

THINK!

Choose the best description for: 'bullying'. Find examples in Chapter One of bullying or cruelty.

1. ☐ Frightening or hurting a person because you think they are smaller or weaker.
2. ☐ Punishing a person because they have done something wrong.
3. ☐ Being horrible to a sister, brother or friend when they make you angry.

Is anyone kind or friendly to Jane in Chapter One?

> **The text and beyond** • page 78
> **Values & Feelings** • page 110

CHAPTER 2

School days

It was a cold January morning. I held tightly to Bessie's neck before saying goodbye. Bessie helped me to take the luggage outside. The coachman stopped briefly and put my parcels on the top of the coach. He didn't have time to wait. We had many miles to travel.

I watched from the windows as the towns became villages, and the villages became open countryside. Several hours later, I heard a voice. A lady shook me gently. 'Jane Eyre?' she asked.

I had fallen asleep. Outside of the coach it was dark and gloomy.[1] There was a strong wind and it was raining hard. In the distance, I saw some grey stone buildings.

Lowood School was very large, but it was very different from Mrs Reed's house. It was cold and forbidding.[2] A teacher took me into a wide, long room which was full of girls. There were about eighty

---

1. **gloomy :** dark and unwelcoming.
2. **forbidding :** frightening, not welcoming.

CHAPTER 2

of them. Their ages were from about nine to twenty. They all wore ugly brown dresses.

It was time for supper.[3] There was only water to drink and a small piece of bread to eat. I drank some water because I was thirsty, but I was too tired to eat anything. After supper, I went upstairs to bed with the other girls. The teacher took me into a very large room with many beds in it. All the girls had to sleep in this one room and there were two girls in every bed.

It was very early when I woke up next morning. It was dark outside and the big room was very cold. We had to wash ourselves in ice-cold water, and then put on our brown dresses. Then we went downstairs to the classroom for the start of the early morning lessons.

I was very hungry and it seemed a long time before it was time for breakfast. There was a terrible smell of burnt food. All of the girls were hungry, but the food was too badly burnt for us to eat. We all left the dining room feeling cold and miserable.

---

3. supper : small meal eaten in the evening.

School days

Lessons began again at nine o'clock. I looked at the other girls and thought how strange they seemed in their ugly brown dresses. Some of the girls were almost young women, and the dresses looked even more odd[4] on these big girls. I did not like the teachers. They seemed to be very strict and unfriendly.

Miss Temple, the head teacher, came in to see us at twelve o'clock. Her face was very pretty and she seemed to be kinder than the other teachers. 'I have something to say to you all,' she said.

'I know that you could not eat your breakfast this morning, so I have decided that you will have bread and cheese for lunch.'

The other teachers looked surprised. 'I'll pay for this meal myself,' Miss Temple told us. The girls were all delighted.[5]

After we had eaten our lunch, we went out into the garden. It was very cold and our brown school dresses were too thin to keep us warm in the winter weather. Nearly all of the girls looked cold

---

4. **odd :** strange.
5. **delighted :** very happy.

and unhappy. Some of them looked very ill. I walked around the garden and hoped that someone would speak to me, but no one did.

One girl was reading a book, and I decided to try to be friendly with her. 'Is your book interesting?' I asked.

'I like it,' she replied.

'Does Miss Temple own the school?' I asked.

'No, she doesn't,' the girl answered. 'A man called Mr Brocklehurst owns the school. People give money to help the school but Mr Brocklehurst buys all our food and clothes.'

This girl was called Helen Burns. I liked her immediately, even though she was older than me. I knew that she would be my friend.

I asked Helen a lot of questions about the school. She told me that often the girls used to become unwell because they did not get enough to eat, and they were always cold.

Mr Brocklehurst was not a generous man. He bought clothes for the girls which were not warm enough for the cold winter, and there was never enough food to eat. Only very strong girls could stay well when they had to live in these hard conditions.

In the spring of that year, many of the girls became ill. They had a disease which was infectious [6] and some of them died.

Lessons stopped, and we girls who were well spent most of our time outside in the fields near the school. The weather was now

---

6. infectious : can be passed from one person to another.

School days

warm and sunny, so it was a happy time for us. My friend, Helen Burns, was not with us. She was so ill that she had to stay in bed.

Miss Temple moved Helen into her own room, and one evening I went to see her. I felt great sadness when I saw how thin she was, and how pale her face had become. When she spoke to me, her voice was so low that I had to come close to her to hear what she said.

'Jane,' she said, 'it's so good to see you. I want to say goodbye.'
'Why, Helen?' I asked her, 'Are you going away from here?'
'Yes, I am, Jane,' Helen replied. 'I'm going far away.'
I stayed with Helen through the night to comfort her, and in the morning I found that she had died.

As a result of so many pupils dying at the school, there was an inquiry[7] into the conditions which had caused the disease. When people knew about the poor food, the dirty water and light clothing which the children were given, they gave money to improve[8] the lives of the girls. Lowood School was a much happier and healthier place from that time on.

---

7. **inquiry :** an official investigation.
8. **improve :** get better.

THINK!

In Chapter Two, Miss Temple buys food when the girls are hungry and moves Helen into her room when she is sick. She could be called a 'role model'. Tick the sentences that are true about role models.

1 ☐ A person that behaves like they care about others, but in fact they don't care.
2 ☐ A person that shows good qualities and is a natural leader.
3 ☐ A person that others respect and want to copy their behaviour.

The text and beyond • page 80
Values & Feelings • page 110

CHAPTER 3

Life as a governess

I stayed for eight more years at Lowood School. I studied hard. Miss Temple taught me drawing and French and I quickly became good at many subjects. For the last two years I worked as a teacher. Miss Temple became like a mother, a governess and then my close friend. Sometimes I would take tea in her room and we would speak of Helen and old times.

One day Miss Temple left the school to marry a clergyman. I felt very alone. I spent the summer painting the countryside around Lowood: the hills, the rivers, the trees, the road I had travelled all those years ago. But I felt restless.[1] I needed a change.

I decided to advertise in a newspaper for a job as a governess. I waited a long time for an answer. Then, at last, I received a letter

---

1. **restless**: not able to relax or be still.

Life as a governess

from a lady, Mrs Fairfax, who lived at a place called Thornfield Hall. She wanted a governess for a little girl. I packed all my things into a small bag, and set out to start a new life.

I was very excited when I first saw the house in which I was going to work. It was very large, but it seemed very quiet. Mrs Fairfax was waiting for me at the door. She was an old lady with a kind face.

'I am pleased to see you, Miss Eyre,' said Mrs Fairfax. 'You must be tired after such a long journey. Sit down and rest. You will meet Adèle later.'

'Is Adèle my student?' I asked.

'Yes, she is nine years old. She is a little French girl, and Mr Rochester wants you to teach her English.'

'Who is Mr Rochester?' I asked.

'Mr Rochester owns Thornfield,' she replied. 'I only work here. I am the housekeeper.'

'Where is Mr Rochester now?' I asked.

'He is away,' she said. 'He does not come very often to Thornfield. I never know when he will return.'

Next day I met Adèle. She was a very pretty little girl and at first, I talked to her in French. I began to teach her English and I was glad that she enjoyed her lessons. I liked Adèle and I liked Mrs Fairfax, too. I was happy at Thornfield, although it was very quiet.

Sometimes I was a little bored, but everyone was very kind to me.

One afternoon I walked to the village to post a letter for Mrs Fairfax. It was winter and the weather was very cold. There was ice on the road. As I walked back to Thornfield Hall, I heard the sound of a horse on the road behind me. I stood to the side of the road to let the horse go past. The rider did not see me.

He was a stranger with dark hair. Suddenly the horse slipped and fell down on the ice.

CHAPTER 3

The man was lying in the road. As I ran forward to help, he struggled[2] to get up.

'Are you hurt, sir?' I asked.

For a moment, the stranger was not able to answer me. Then he looked at me in surprise.

'Can I do anything to help?' I asked again.

'You can stand on one side while I catch my horse,' he replied.

But the horse managed to get up by itself, and I realised that it was the stranger himself who was hurt. He tried to stand up, but his injured leg was hurting too much. I helped him to get back onto his horse, and he rode away without thanking me.

'Who is he?' I asked myself. 'He is not very handsome and not at all polite, but he looks interesting.

I would like to know him.'

When I arrived back at Thornfield, everyone was very excited and busy. I asked Mrs Fairfax what was happening.

'Mr Rochester has returned,' she said. 'But he may go away again soon. He wants to see you and Adèle, Miss Eyre. Go and put on your best dress. He will see you after dinner.'

After dinner, I took Adèle to see Mr Rochester in his room.

When I entered the room, I stopped in surprise and stared at the man who was sitting in the chair. It was the man who had fallen from his horse. The interesting stranger was Mr Rochester!

Mr Rochester decided to stay at Thornfield for a while.[3] He was busy all day, but sometimes he talked to me in the evening.

He did not smile or laugh very often. He enjoyed asking me questions and watching me try to answer them. At first, I could not understand him and I found him quite rude but in time I saw that

---

2. struggle : try very hard.
3. a while : some time.

CHAPTER 3

he was also a very gentle and intelligent man. I was happy when I was with him and I began to enjoy his company.

One night, quite some time after I had gone to bed, I woke up suddenly.

It was very early in the morning. I thought that I heard something unusual. Everything was silent, but I listened very carefully, and I heard the sound again. Someone was moving about outside my room.

'Is anyone there?' I called. There was no answer. I felt worried and very frightened. But the house was silent again, and after a while, I tried to go back to sleep. But then I heard a laugh. It was a terrible, cruel sound, which made me quite cold with fear.

There was a sound of footsteps[4] walking away, and going up the steps to the attic. I could not sleep after that. I put on my clothes and went to find Mrs Fairfax. I heard nothing now, but suddenly I realised that I could smell smoke. It was coming from Mr Rochester's bedroom. I ran into the room and saw that his bed was on fire. I tried to wake him, but he did not move. I looked around the room, looking for something to put out the fire.

I saw a large jug[5] of water on a small table. I picked it up and threw the water onto the burning bed. Then, Mr Rochester woke up.

---

4. footsteps : the noise feet make when they touch the ground.
5. jug : container for water.

Life as a governess

'What's happening?' he cried. 'Is that you, Jane? What is wrong?'

'You must get up, Mr Rochester,' I said. 'Your bed was on fire, but I have put it out[6] now.'

He got out of bed quickly. The water was everywhere and there was still smoke from the fire.

'Jane, you have saved my life,' he said. 'What made you wake up? How did you know about the fire?'

I told him about the noise I had heard outside my room and the strange laugh.

Mr Rochester looked upset and angry. 'I must go upstairs to the attic,' he told me. 'Stay here and wait for me. Do not leave the room. Don't tell anyone what has happened.'

I waited in the room for a long time. At last, Mr Rochester came back. 'Go back to bed now, Jane,' he said. 'Everything is all right. You are quite safe.'

Next day, I asked Mrs Fairfax, 'Who lives in the attic?'

'A woman called Grace Poole,' she answered. 'She is one of the servants. She's a little strange.'

I remembered Grace Poole. She was a large, silent woman who did not speak to the other servants in the house. Perhaps it was Grace Poole who wandered[7] around the house at night, and laughed outside my door?

In the evening, when Adèle had finished her lessons, I went to talk to Mrs Fairfax.

'Mr Rochester left the house early today,' she told me. 'He says that he is going to stay with friends. He didn't say when he will come back.'

The house was very quiet while he was away. Mr Rochester stayed

---

6. put it out : extinguish it.
7. wander : move around without any clear direction.

CHAPTER 3

with his friends for a few weeks, and I continued to teach Adèle her lessons. I did not hear the strange laugh again.

When I returned from a walk one day, I found that Mrs Fairfax and the servants were very excited. Mrs Fairfax showed me a letter which she had received from Mr Rochester. 'He is coming back tomorrow,' she said. 'He is bringing some of his friends with him. We are going to be very busy with so many visitors in the house. Miss Blanche Ingram is coming, too. She is very beautiful and very rich.'

Mr Rochester and his friends arrived the next day. Mrs Fairfax was right when she said that Miss Ingram was beautiful. But she was proud [8] too, and didn't seem to notice me.

I was too poor and unimportant. But she was very interested in Mr Rochester. They talked a lot together, and often went horse riding. One night they sang together. Blanche was enchanting [9] and Mr Rochester sung in a beautiful deep voice.

'Do you think that Mr Rochester might marry Miss Ingram?' I asked Mrs Fairfax when we were in her room afterwards.

She looked up for a moment from her sewing. 'He might. But she is young,' she added. I decided to change the subject.

---

8. proud : thought she was better than other people.
9. enchanting : very pleasant (to listen to).

THINK!

In Chapter Three, Jane shows she can be courageous. Tick the sentences that show this.

1. ☐ She decides to start a new life in a place she has never been.
2. ☐ She goes to post a letter on her own and helps a stranger on the road.
3. ☐ She is frightened after hearing a terrible laugh and can't sleep.
4. ☐ She puts out a fire and saves Mr Rochester's life.

| **The text and beyond** • page 82
| **Values & Feelings** • page 110

CHAPTER 4

The incident in the attic

The next few weeks were happy ones at Thornfield Hall. There was music and dancing. The guests played games like billiards and charades.[1] The longer I stayed at Thornfield Hall, the closer I felt to my master. Of course, I had to remind myself not to show these feelings. If Mr Rochester married Miss Ingram, he might decide to send Adèle to school. He wouldn't need me as his governess. I held Adèle tight when I thought about this.

One evening Adèle saw a carriage arriving. She ran excitedly to the window to see who it was. I looked out of the window and saw a stranger. He was a well-dressed man with dark hair.

---

1. charades : a game in which the players try to communicate a word without speaking.

The incident in the attic

He said that his name was Mr Mason and that he and Mr Rochester were old friends. But Mr Rochester looked alarmed[2] when he saw him. His face turned[3] white.

Mr Rochester and Mr Mason talked for a long time that night. They went to bed very late.

I woke up suddenly and heard a terrible scream from the room above my bedroom. Then there was a lot of noise, as if people were fighting. There was another loud scream.

'Help!' I heard a voice shout. 'Rochester! Come quickly! Help me!'

I heard doors opening and the sound of someone running. I put on my clothes and opened my door. All the visitors were awake and standing outside their doors.

'What's happened?' they cried. 'Is there a fire? Who screamed?'

Mr Rochester came down the stairs from the attic. His friends crowded around him, asking him questions. 'Everything is all right,' he told them.

'But we heard such a terrible noise,' said Miss Ingram. 'One of the servants had a nightmare,' he explained to them. 'That is all. She's a very nervous person. She thought that she saw a ghost, and so she screamed. Please go back to bed now. There is no need to worry.'

2. **alarmed :** afraid and worried.
3. **turn :** (here) become.

CHAPTER 4

One by one, the ladies and Mr Rochester's friends went back to their rooms.

I also went back to my room, but soon afterwards someone knocked at my door. I opened it and saw Mr Rochester.

'Jane, can you come with me?' he asked. I knew from his voice that something was very wrong.

'Yes, of course,' I said, and I followed him down the corridor and up the stairs to the attic. He unlocked the door of the attic and we entered the room.

'Wait here,' he said. I stayed outside the door of another room, while he unlocked it and went inside.

Then from behind this door I heard a terrible sound. It sounded like a wounded[4] animal, crying with rage.[5]

Once again, I heard that cruel, frightening laugh. Was Grace Poole inside that room? Mr Rochester came out and locked the door again. 'Are you afraid of the sight of blood, Jane?' he asked me.

'I don't think so,' I replied.

'Then come into the room with me,' he said.

I entered the room and saw that Mr Mason was lying on a large bed. His face was pale and his eyes were closed. His white shirt was covered in blood.

'Is he dead?' I asked.

'No,' Mr Rochester replied. 'He isn't badly hurt, but I must go and call a doctor for him. Will you stay with him until I return?'

Mr Mason moved and tried to speak. Mr Rochester said to him, 'Don't try to talk, Mason. You must not speak to Jane while I am away.'

Mr Rochester left me alone with the injured man. He was away for a long time and I was very frightened. Grace Poole was in the

---

4. wounded : injured.
5. rage : great anger.

next room, and at any moment she might come in and try to hurt Mr Mason or me.

After a very long time, Mr Rochester came back with the doctor. Mr Rochester said to me, 'Thank you for your help, Jane.

Mason is now going to leave Thornfield Hall. The doctor will take him away and care for him in a safe place.'

I helped Mr Rochester and the doctor to get Mr Mason down the stairs and out of the house.

'Take care of him, doctor,' said Mr Rochester. 'Soon he will be well enough to go back to the West Indies.'

But before he got into the carriage, Mr Mason said something very strange. 'Look after her, Rochester. Promise to look after her.'

'Yes,' said Mr Rochester, and his face was very sad. 'I will always look after her.'

I wanted to go back to the house and to my bed, but Mr Rochester put his hand on my arm.

'Don't go yet,' he said. 'Walk with me for a while.'

We walked together in the garden.

CHAPTER 4

'What a night that was,' Mr Rochester said. 'Were you afraid, Jane?'

'Yes, I was,' I replied. 'While I waited for you in the attic, I heard something in the next room... I heard a terrible laugh. Was it Grace Poole, Mr Rochester? Will she go away now?'

'Don't worry about Grace Poole,' he said. He did not look at me as he spoke. 'She will not harm⁶ you. It is Mason I fear. I will not be happy until he is back in the West Indies.'

'But Mr Mason is a quiet and gentle man,' I said, surprised.

'I'm sure that he will do what you tell him.'

'No, he'll not hurt me knowingly,' Mr Rochester replied. 'But he might say something without meaning⁷ to, which would do me great harm.'

I was surprised when I heard this. 'Then you must tell him to be careful about what he says,' I said.

Mr Rochester turned to look at me. He smiled softly. There was both a tenderness⁸ and a sadness in his eyes that I could not explain.

'It is not that simple, Jane,' he said. 'I wish it was!'

We returned to the house together in silence.

---

6. **harm** : (here) cause physical injury.
7. **meaning** : (here) intending.
8. **tenderness** : kind and gentle feelings.

THINK!

Jane and Mr Rochester have become closer. Think about the value of friendship. Which of these are important in a friendship? Does one person behave more like a friend?

being a good listener   having a similar social position
not having secrets   sharing feelings   showing respect
being patient   having the same interests   knowing the same people

---

▎ **The text and beyond** • page 84
▎ **Values & Feelings** • page 110

CHAPTER 5

Surprising news

One morning Mrs Fairfax asked me to come downstairs to the study. A coachman was waiting for me.

'You don't remember me, do you miss?' he said. 'But I think you remember Bessie.'

'Bessie? The maid at Mrs Reed's house? Of course, I remember her. Is she well?' I asked, a little worried by this visit.

'Yes, Bessie is well. She is now my wife. We have two children and they are growing up quickly. I'm afraid the news is about Mrs Reed. Your cousin John died suddenly. It was a great shock to your aunt. She is very ill. She asked to see you especially. We looked everywhere. We didn't think we would find you until someone at Lowood School gave us this address.'

CHAPTER 5

Even though I was surprised that my aunt wished to see me, I couldn't say no to this request. I asked Mrs Fairfax to explain my departure to Mr Rochester and I set off at once.

When I arrived, I saw that my aunt was very ill. At first, she could not speak to me.

But one day, as I was sitting by her bed, she showed me a letter. It was from my father's brother, who lived in Madeira.[1] This is what it said.

Dear Mrs Reed,

I am looking for my brother's daughter, Jane Eyre. I am now a rich man, and I have no children of my own. I want Jane Eyre to live with me. Can you help me to find my niece?

Yours sincerely,

John Eyre

I looked at the date on the letter. 'But, Mrs Reed,' I said, 'this letter was sent three years ago. Why didn't you tell me about it before?'

'I never liked you, Jane Eyre,' my aunt replied. 'I wrote a letter to your uncle and I told him that you were dead. I told him you died at Lowood School. Now go away and leave me.'

A few days afterwards, Mrs Reed died. I felt sad that she had disliked me until her death, and I felt glad to leave her house and return to Thornfield Hall.

It was summer and the fields around Thornfield were very green and full of flowers. For me it was the most beautiful place in the world because it was now my home.

---

1. Madeira : an island in the Atlantic Ocean off the north-west coast of Africa. It was a colony of Portugal.

CHAPTER 5

'I know that Adèle will be pleased to see me,' I thought. 'But what about Mr Rochester? I want to see him so much, but how does he feel about me? Perhaps he is already married to Blanche Ingram? What if they are going to marry soon? What will I do?' I felt unhappy when I thought about Mr Rochester and Blanche Ingram. 'I can't stay here when they are married,' I thought. 'I must leave this house, which I love, and I will never see Mr Rochester again.'

When I came near the house, I saw Mr Rochester. He was pleased to see me and so were Mrs Fairfax and Adèle. I really felt that I had come back home.

One evening, a few weeks afterwards, I went for a walk in the garden after I had finished teaching Adèle. Mr Rochester saw me there. 'Come and talk to me, Jane,' he said.

'He's going to tell me that he is going to marry Blanche Ingram,' I thought.

'Are you happy here, Jane?' he asked.

'Yes, Mr Rochester, I am very happy,' I replied.

'You'll be sad to leave here,' he said.

I could not look at him. 'He is going to tell me that I must leave because he's getting married,' I thought.

'Yes, I will be very sad to leave,' I said.

'But you must leave, Jane,' Mr Rochester said.

'Must I?' I asked. 'Would I need to go soon?'

'Yes, you would need to go soon,' he said.

'Is it because you are going to get married?' I asked.

'Yes, Jane, I am going to get married. Adèle must go to school and you must find a new job. I will help you. It will be far from here, though, my little friend.'

'Then I shall never see you again?' I cried.

'You'll soon forget me when you are far away,' he answered.

Surprising news

'But I will never forget you,' I thought. 'You may forget me, when I am not here, but I will never forget you, Mr Rochester.'

I could hardly speak. Tears were in my eyes and all that I could say was, 'Never!'

He looked at me for a long time and then, at last, he spoke.

'Perhaps you don't need to go,' he said. 'Perhaps you can stay here when I am married.'

I felt angry now. Did this man think I was made of stone? Did he not know how I felt? Did he even care how much his words hurt me?

'I could never stay,' I told him. 'When Miss Ingram is your wife, I must go. I know that I am not rich and beautiful like her. I am poor and unimportant. But I still feel sadness. If you marry Miss Ingram, I must leave here.'

I was surprised when Mr Rochester smiled. 'But I don't want you to go, Jane,' he said. 'I am not going to marry Miss Ingram. Please stay here with me, because it's you I want to marry.'

CHAPTER 5

I heard what he said but I could not believe it. 'You are laughing at me,' I said. 'How can you be so cruel?'

'I am not laughing at you, Jane,' he answered.

'But I don't understand! What about Miss Ingram?'

'She never loved me, Jane, and I didn't love her. Her uncle wanted her to find a good match and he thought it might bring him more money. But I told him his family would never have my money. I'm sorry I made you believe I was going to marry her. I just wanted you to see how you felt. Is that so wrong? It is you I want to marry, not Miss Ingram… Jane, will you marry me?'

He looked at me so tenderly[2] that I had to believe him. Mr Rochester wanted me, Jane Eyre, to be his wife!

'Yes,' I said quietly, 'I will marry you.'

'We will be happy, Jane. No one is going to stop us,' he told me, with a strange look in his eyes, which I did not quite understand. But I was too happy at that moment to think about it for long.

It began to get dark. The weather changed and a strong wind started to blow. Rain started to fall as we walked back to the house together.

2. **tenderly :** with much love.

THINK!

Find the word 'forgiveness' in a dictionary. Think about Jane's relationship with Mrs Reed and the value of forgiveness. Answer the questions.

1. Why did Jane go to see her Aunt?
2. Why did Mrs Reed show Jane the letter?
3. Did she apologise or ask Jane to forgive her?

The text and beyond • page 86
Values & Feelings • page 110

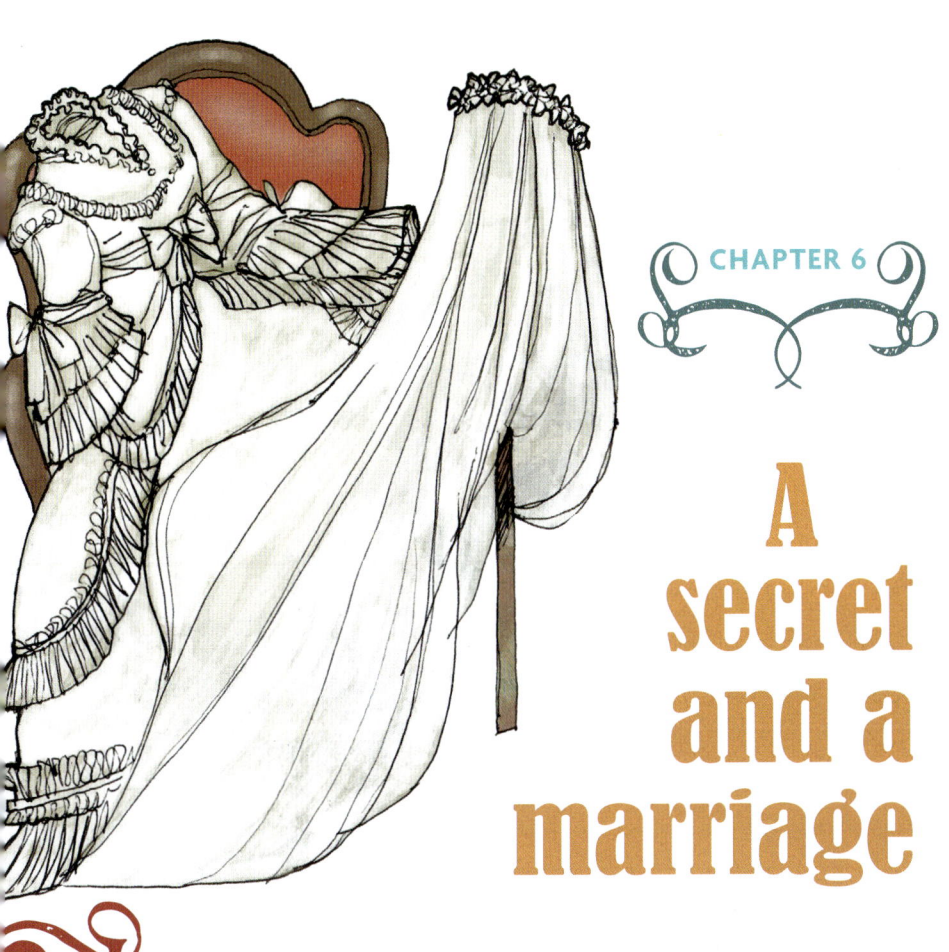

CHAPTER 6

A secret and a marriage

I spent the next month in complete happiness and anxiety. Mrs Fairfax said I should be careful. 'You are his governess,' she reminded me. 'Be sure that he cares about you.' But nothing could change my feelings. I knew now what it was to love someone and to be loved by someone else.

Mr Rochester wanted to buy me a necklace and an expensive dress but I refused them. I chose a simple dress and a veil[1] instead.

I was aware[2] that I had no money. I would never be rich like he was but maybe if I wrote to my uncle in Madeira. At least then,

---

1. **veil :** thin piece of material covering the head/face (here: worn with a wedding dress.)
2. **aware :** to know and understand something.

I would have had a relation. I felt sure my uncle would be happy that I was still alive.

Two nights before the wedding, I was asleep in my room. My wedding dress was in the room with me. The night was windy and the wind made a strange noise. Suddenly, I woke up. There was a light in my room. I thought at first that it was morning, but when I looked at the window I saw that it was still dark outside.

Someone was in my room. Was it Mrs Fairfax or Grace Poole? It was a woman, but a woman I had never seen before. She was big, tall and strong. Her black hair was long and thick. She was dressed

in a long, white garment.³ I could not see her face. She held my wedding dress and veil up in front of her. She looked at her reflection in the mirror and it was then that I saw her face! It was the most terrible face. She had large, red eyes and her skin was purple. She looked angry and dangerous and I felt terrified by the sight of her.

Then she took my veil and tore it to pieces.⁴ She threw the pieces down on the floor and went over to look out of the window. Then she turned and started to come towards my bed. I was so frightened

---

3. garment : (here) a long dress; piece of clothing.
4. tear it to pieces : rip, pull into pieces.

CHAPTER 6

that I was unable to move. I couldn't even scream for help. 'She is going to kill me,' I thought. But then the light disappeared, and the room was dark once more.

I woke up in the morning. The sun was shining in through the window, and at once I remembered the strange woman. I thought at first that I had had a bad dream. Then I saw my ruined[5] veil, lying on the floor, torn to pieces. It was true! The strange woman was real!

Mr Rochester looked very worried and was silent for a long time when I told him about the woman, but he just said, 'You had a bad dream, Jane. It was probably Grace Poole who tore your veil, but you dreamt that it was a stranger.'

I could not believe that the strange woman had been just a dream, but I said nothing. That night, the night before the wedding, I slept in Adèle's room.

The next day, we went to the church for the wedding. In the church, while the clergyman was speaking, someone threw open the church door and said, 'Stop the wedding! It cannot go on. Mr Rochester already has a wife. He is married to this man's sister!'

All the people in the church turned to see who was speaking. It was a small man with round glasses. He introduced himself as Mr Briggs. He said he was a lawyer. Then behind him I saw Mr Mason, the visitor from the West Indies. What was he talking about? How could Mr Rochester be married? My heart turned cold. I could not believe that this was happening on my wedding day.

'But where is Mr Rochester's wife?' asked the clergyman. 'Why haven't we seen her?'

'She lives at Thornfield Hall,' Mr Mason replied. 'She is alive. I saw her recently.'

---

5. ruined : so damaged it could not be repaired.

Mr Rochester struggled to speak. His face was white and distressed.[6] At last he said, 'It is true. My wife is living at Thornfield Hall. We were married fifteen years ago in the West Indies, when we were both young. Her name is Bertha Mason, and she is Mason's sister. Soon after we were married, she changed. She became very strange and then she became mad and dangerous. She attacked me and anyone who came near her. Last April, she tried to kill her own brother.

'She has a nurse, Grace Poole, who looks after her at Thornfield. I have told no one else that she is my wife. This young woman, Jane Eyre, knows nothing about her.' Mr Rochester's face was sad. 'Come with me and I will take you to see her.'

---

6. distressed : agitated, tormented.

CHAPTER 6

We were all silent as we walked from the church back to Thornfield Hall. Mr Rochester took us up to the attic and unlocked the door. Grace Poole was there, and in the room, too, was the frightening, terrible woman that I had seen in my bedroom. She was the person who had the cruel laugh. She was the one who had set fire to Mr Rochester's bed, who had tried to kill Mr Mason and who had ruined my veil. Yes, she was mad, but she was also Mr Rochester's wife. I knew that I could not marry him.

Although I felt sorry for Mr Rochester, I knew that I must leave my home, Thornfield Hall, for ever. I put a few clothes into a small bag. I took a little money, and quietly left Thornfield Hall early the next morning. I told no one that I was going, and no one saw me leave.

THINK!

Think about values that are important in a marriage. Find any new words. Then number the values in order of importance to you. Add some of your own.

- [ ] love
- [ ] trust
- [ ] good communication
- [ ] being generous
- [ ] making sacrifices
- [ ] keeping promises
- [ ] compassion
- [ ] obedience
- [ ] forgiveness

Does Mr Rochester show any of these in his marriage? In your opinion, should he be allowed to get a divorce and marry Jane?

The text and beyond • page 88
Values & Feelings • page 110

CHAPTER 7

A new life

I walked for many miles until Mr Rochester and Thornfield Hall were a good distance away. Finally, I saw a coach. I gave the coachman almost all the money I had to take me as far as he could. After two days and nights, I arrived at a very isolated[1] place. There were no towns or villages, just a few houses beyond a hill. The coach drove away quickly. I shouted after it, but it was too late. I had left a small bag with all my possessions inside the coach. I had nothing. I was cold, hungry and exhausted.[2] There was an old signpost and a crossroads so I took the path towards the hill and prepared myself for the long journey ahead.

---

1. **isolated :** a long way from any people or places.
2. **exhausted :** very tired (almost ill).

A new life

As night fell I saw the light of a house in the distance. I came closer and looked through the window. There were two young women in the room. I thought that they looked kind, so I knocked on the door. It was opened by a servant.

'Who are you?' she asked. 'What do you want?'

'I'm alone in the world and I have no money or food,' I told her. 'I'm tired and hungry. Please, can you help me?'

The servant stared at me. She did not look very friendly. 'I'll give you some bread,' she said. 'But then you must go. You can't stay here.' She came back and gave me the bread, and said, 'Now go away.'

I was too tired to move. I sat down outside the door of the house. 'There is no one to help me,' I said. 'I will die here.'

I didn't know that someone was watching and listening to me.

'You are not going to die,' a voice said. A tall, handsome young man was looking down at me. 'Who are you?' He knocked on the door and the servant opened it again.

'Who is this young woman, Hannah?' he asked.

CHAPTER 7

'I don't know, sir,' the servant replied. 'I gave her some bread and told her to go away.'

'She can't go away, Hannah,' the young man said. 'She is too ill. We must take her inside and help her.'

They took me into the house, where it was warm and comfortable. The two young women asked me my name. 'I am Jane Elliott,' I told them. I didn't want to tell them my real name in case Mr Rochester tried to find me. I wanted to start a new life.

My kind new friends took me upstairs to a bedroom, where I slept for a very long time. When I woke up, I felt much better.

I was soon well enough to talk to the people who had been so kind to me. The names of the two young women were Diana and Mary Rivers. The young man was their brother and his name was St John Rivers. He was a clergyman. He had fair hair and blue eyes and was very good looking. But his face was always serious and he did not often laugh or smile. He planned to go to India to work.

A new life

Diana and Mary were much friendlier than their brother, but I didn't want to tell them about Mr Rochester. 'I have no family of my own,' I said. 'My parents are dead. I went to Lowood School and after I left I went to work as a governess. I had to leave suddenly, but I have done nothing wrong. Please believe me.'

'Don't worry, Jane, we believe you,' said Diana. 'Don't talk any more now. You are tired.'

'You will want to find some work,' said St John.

'Yes, and as soon as possible,' I replied.

'Good,' he said. 'Then I will help you.'

Diana and Mary went back to work at their teaching jobs in the south of England soon afterwards. St John asked me to teach the children who lived near his church. The school was very small and the children were very poor, but I enjoyed my work.

I lived in a small cottage near the school. I did not have much money, and I saw very few people, but St John often came to see me, and gave me books to read. My life was very quiet, but I was happy, except for when I thought about Mr Rochester. I knew that I would always love him.

THINK!

Think about how Jane feels when she arrives at the Rivers' House. Unscramble the letters to describe her feelings.

a xadesuhte **b** nughyr **c** rfadai **d** ewka **e** olnyel **f** fere

Think about the values of compassion and understanding.

1 Who shows compassion?
2 Does everyone show compassion?
3 Is compassion the same as friendship?
4 Do Diana and Maria show trust and understanding?

> **The text and beyond** • page 90
> **Values & Feelings** • page 110

An unexpected proposal

In the months that came, I was too busy to be lonely. My pupils were poor but they were quick to learn. The school was successful and I was soon made to feel welcome in the village. One of my few pleasures from my days at Lowood was to draw and paint. Diana and Mary kindly gave me paints and coloured pencils. In my paintings, I escaped to new worlds. I drew beautiful scenes from nature. Sometimes I drew people, too.

One evening, St John came to my house to see me when I was just finishing painting a picture. He looked closely at some of my other pictures. Then he tore a piece of paper off the bottom of one of the pictures and put it in his pocket. I waited for him to say something, but he remained silent. 'How strange he is,' I thought.

Even though it snowed the next day, and the weather was very cold, St John came to see me again.

I was very surprised to see him.

'Why are you here?' I asked him. 'Has something bad happened? Are your sisters all right?'

'Don't worry,' he said. 'Diana and Mary are both well.'

St John sat down beside the fire and said nothing for a long time. I wondered[1] what had made him come to see me on such a cold, dark night.

At last, he spoke.

'Jane, I know your story,' he told me. 'I know about your parents, and Mrs Reed. I know about your time at Lowood and about Mr Rochester. I also know about Mr Rochester's wife. I know why you came here with no money. Mr Rochester must be a very bad man,' he said.

'No, no!' I cried. 'He isn't bad.'

'I have had a letter from a man in London, called Mr Briggs, who is looking for someone called Jane Eyre,' St John said. 'You say that your name is Jane Elliott, but I know that you are Jane Eyre. Look!' He showed me the piece

---

1. wonder : ask myself.

of paper from the bottom of my painting. My real name, Jane Eyre, was on it.

'Mr Briggs,' I repeated quietly. Suddenly everything made sense. I thought about the letter to my uncle before the wedding. Mr Briggs was Mr Mason's lawyer. 'Does Mr Briggs know anything about Mr Rochester?' I asked. 'Does he know how Mr Rochester is?'

I could only think about Mr Rochester, because I still loved him.

'Mr Briggs said nothing about Mr Rochester,' said St John.

'This letter was about your uncle, Mr Eyre of Madeira. Mr Eyre is dead. He left you all his money. You are very rich, Jane.' I was so surprised that I was unable to speak for a long time. I did not feel excited or happy. Instead, I wondered what it would mean to be rich.

'I don't understand,' I said, when I was able to speak again.
'Why did Mr Briggs write to you?'
'Because,' said St John, 'Mr Eyre of Madeira was my mother's brother, which means that he is also our uncle.'
'Then you and your sisters are my cousins,' I said, feeling happy now. 'We can share the money between the four of us. Diana and Mary can come home, and we can all live together.'
It was good to have money, after being poor for all of my life, but it was even better to know that I had three cousins.
Diana and Mary came home just before Christmas. I worked happily to make their old house comfortable.
'I know that Diana and Mary will like it,' I thought. 'But what will St John think? He is such a strange man. He's hard and cold, like

CHAPTER 8

a stone. Even though he's pleased to see his sisters, he does not look really happy.'

I soon realised that St John was not content with just having money. He still wanted to go to India. I was happy living with Diana and Mary, but I still thought about Mr Rochester every day. Was he still at Thornfield? Was he happy? I had to know, so I wrote to the lawyer, Mr Briggs. Mr Briggs replied that he knew nothing about Mr Rochester. I wrote to Mrs Fairfax at Thornfield Hall, but there was no reply.

When a letter came for me at last, it was from Mr Briggs about the money. I was so disappointed that I started to cry.

St John came into the room while I was crying. 'Jane, come for a walk with me,' he said. 'I want to talk to you.'

We walked together beside the river. St John was very quiet at first, but then he turned and said to me, 'Jane, I'm going to India soon, and I want you to come with me.'

I was very surprised by what he said. Why did he want me to go to India with him? How could I help him?

I was not strong like he was.

'I don't think I would be a very good helper for you, St John...' I began to say.

'No, not as a helper. I want you to be my wife. If we get married, we can work together in India. There are many poor people there who need our help.'

It was hard to believe what St John was saying to me.

'I can't work in India. I don't know how to help the poor people there. I'm not like you, St John.'

'That doesn't matter,'² St John replied. 'I shall tell you what to do. You will soon learn. I saw how hard you worked in the village school.

---

2. doesn't matter : isn't important.

An unexpected proposal

I know that you will work hard in India, too.' I said nothing while I thought about what St John had said. He was my cousin and he needed my help. He was going to do good and useful work in India. Maybe I should do as he asked?

'If I help you, then I must be free,' I said. 'You are like a brother to me. I can't marry you.'

St John's face looked like stone. 'No, Jane! You must be my wife. There is a lot of good work we can both do in India but I do not need

CHAPTER 8

a sister, I need a wife. Think of the difference you could make to your life and ours.'

I turned away from St John so that he could not see how upset I was. I was confused. I remembered my love for Mr Rochester. He was so kind and gentle when he spoke to me. St John spoke coldly to me. He told me he wanted a wife but I did not feel that he loved me. What could I say to him?

'I am going away for two weeks, to visit friends,' said St John.

'When I return, I will want to know your answer. I hope that you will agree to marry me. It is the right thing for you to do, Jane. You can't stay here forever, doing nothing.'

I saw Diana when I went back to the house. When she saw my unhappy face, she asked, 'What is wrong, Jane? You look so pale and upset. What has happened to you?'

'St John has asked me to marry him,' I said, miserably.

'That is wonderful,' Diana cried. 'If you marry him, he will stay here in England with us, instead of going to India.'

'No,' I said. 'He wants me to go to India with him.'

Diana looked surprised. 'But you can't go to India,' she said. 'You're not strong³ enough.'

'I won't go because I can't marry him,' I told her. 'I'm afraid that he's angry with me, Diana. I know that he's a good man, but I don't think that he understands how ordinary people feel.'

'Yes,' Diana said, seriously. 'My brother is a very good man, but sometimes he appears to be hard and cold.'

That night I lay in bed thinking about St John. I could not decide what to do. His work was everything to him. I missed the adventure of doing something new. I could not love St John but maybe he was right.

---

3. strong : (here) in good health.

An unexpected proposal

What would my life become if I stayed in the village? Maybe I should marry him and go to India after all.

The night was very quiet. I could hear nothing in the darkness.

Suddenly, I thought that I heard a voice. 'Jane!' it called, 'Jane! Jane!'

It was Mr Rochester's voice.

'I am here, Mr Rochester.' I cried. 'Where are you? What is wrong?'

Was I dreaming? Perhaps, but it didn't matter. Somehow, I knew that Mr Rochester needed me. 'I must go to him at once,'[4] I thought.

The next day, I left once more for Thornfield Hall.

---

4. at once : immediately.

THINK!

In Chapter Eight Jane feels very confused. Tick the events that makes her feel like this. Think of other events that are surprising or unexpected.

- [ ] She wants the school to be a success but she is in a small village.
- [ ] She receives a lot of money after her Uncle Reed dies.
- [ ] She finds out that the lawyer is Mr Briggs. She has no word of Mr Rochester.
- [ ] St John tells he wants to marry her but he is cold.
- [ ] She hears Mr Rochester's voice and knows she must go to him.

Think about the value of being hard working. Which characters does this adjective describe? Is it always a quality to be hard working? Which words describe a) St John; b) Jane? Do you think they are a good match?

sensible cold serious kind friendly independent
strong determined passionate proud

The text and beyond • page 92
Values & Feelings • page 110

CHAPTER 9

Mr Rochester

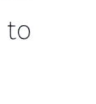

I felt great excitement at the thought of seeing my old home again. 'But what about Mr Rochester? People would know his secret by now. They might know about the wedding, too. Had he left the country? What about his wife?' These thoughts returned to my head often during the long journey back to Thornfield.

'I will stop at the inn¹ first,' I thought. 'Maybe they can give me some news.' But the thought of being disappointed was too much for me. I continued to the house for the last two miles on foot.

The trees and the road were just the same as when I had left. I stood and looked, hoping to see the image that had been in my mind

---

1. inn: a small hotel or pub usually in the country.

Mr Rochester

for so long. Instead, I could not believe what I saw. My beautiful home was in ruins!

No one could live here now. I now knew why Mrs Fairfax never answered my letters. The walls of the house were still standing, but the roof had gone. The windows were dark and empty. The gardens were neglected.[2] The walls of the old house were black. There was no sound except for the song of birds and the noise of the wind. Where was Mrs Fairfax? Where was little Adèle? And where – oh where – was Mr Rochester?

I hurried back to the village and asked a man to tell me what had happened.

'Last autumn, the house burnt down in the middle of the night,' he told me.

'How did it happen?' I asked him.

'People say that Mr Rochester's wife started the fire,' he said.

'No one ever saw the lady, but they say that she was mad. They say she started the fire in the attic, where she lived. Mrs Fairfax was visiting friends when it happened, and the little girl, Adèle, was away at school.'

I stared at the man. I could not believe what he was telling me.

'Mr Rochester didn't want to see anyone at the time,' he said.

'It seems he was very unhappy. He wanted to marry a young girl, but she ran away.'

I felt embarrassed, but he did not seem to know who I was. 'What happened when the fire started?' I asked.

'Mr Rochester got all the servants out of the house,' he continued, 'and then he went back in to save his wife. I saw her standing on the roof. She was waving[3] her arms and shouting.

---

2. **neglect :** not look after.
3. **waving :** moving her arms quickly.

Mr Rochester

Mr Rochester tried to help her, but she would not let him. Suddenly she fell from the roof.'

'Did she die?' I asked.

'Yes, she died at once,' he said. 'And Mr Rochester was badly injured. When he came out of the house, he was blind and he had lost one hand.'

I had been so afraid that the man was going to tell me that Mr Rochester was dead. I began to hope again. He was hurt, but he was still alive!

'Where does Mr Rochester live now?' I asked the man.

'He lives near here, at a quiet little place called Ferndean,' he replied. 'He can't travel far since he was hurt. He lives with just two servants. He never has any visitors.'

CHAPTER 9

I went to Ferndean at once, and arrived there just before dark. When I got near the house, I saw a man come out. I knew at once that it was Mr Rochester. He looked so different from the man I had known. He was still tall and his hair was still dark, but his face was sad. He could not walk without help. After a few minutes, he turned and went slowly back into the house.

I knocked on the door and Mary, a servant, answered it. She recognised me[4] at once. I told her that I had heard about the fire at Thornfield Hall, and about what had happened to Mr Rochester.

'Go to Mr Rochester and tell him that he has a visitor,' I said to Mary. 'But don't tell him who it is.'

'He won't see you, Miss Jane,' she said. 'He has refused to see anyone since the fire.'

I went into the room where Mr Rochester was sitting.

'Is that you, Mary?' he asked. 'Answer me!'

---

4. recognise me : know who I was.

Mr Rochester

'Will you have some water?' I said to him.

'That is Jane Eyre's voice,' Mr Rochester said. 'Jane, is it really you?'

'Yes. It is really me,' I said. 'I've come home to be with you. I'll never leave you again.'

'Oh Jane, why did you go?' he asked. 'Why did you leave so suddenly? Why did you not stay and let me help you?'

'You know why I went,' I said. 'It was the only thing that I could do. But things have changed. I am a rich woman now.'

I told Mr Rochester all about my cousins, and about my new home.

'Then you do not need me now,' he said. 'Will you really stay with me?' There was hope in his voice. I smiled at him, although he could not see me.

'Of course, I will,' I said.

'But you're so young,' he said. 'You don't want to marry me. I'm blind and I can't do anything. You must marry a young man. What is your cousin, St John Rivers, like? Is he young or old?'

'He is young and handsome,' I answered.

'Do you like him?' he asked.

'Yes, I do,' I answered. 'He's a very good man.'

'Does he like you?' he asked.

'Yes, he does,' I answered. 'He wants me to marry him.'

'Will you marry him?' he asked.

'No. I don't love him.' I told him.

Mr Rochester looked happy. He held my hand, and he was silent for a long time. Then, at last he said to me very quietly,

'Jane, may I ask you again now? Will you marry me?'

'Yes, I will marry you,' I said. I was delighted. Mr Rochester looked happier than I had ever seen him.

And this is how my story ends.

CHAPTER 9

Reader, I married him. We had a quiet little wedding. Only the clergyman and a clerk were present.

Diana and Mary were delighted when I wrote to tell them the news. I also wrote to St John, but he never replied. He went to India and did much good work there, but he never married.

Little Adèle came back to live with us when she had finished school. She is now a wonderful friend to me.

Mr Rochester and I have now been married for ten years. Two years after we were married, Mr Rochester began to see again with one eye. He can now see me and our two children.

Our story has been a strange and terrible one. We both suffered[5] greatly before we could be together, but now, at last, we are happy.

---

5. suffer : have difficult experiences.

THINK!

Think about the difference between feelings and values. Complete the puzzle with letters to spell feelings and values. Which word is shaded? Think about how this word might describe Jane and Mr Rochester's relationship now.

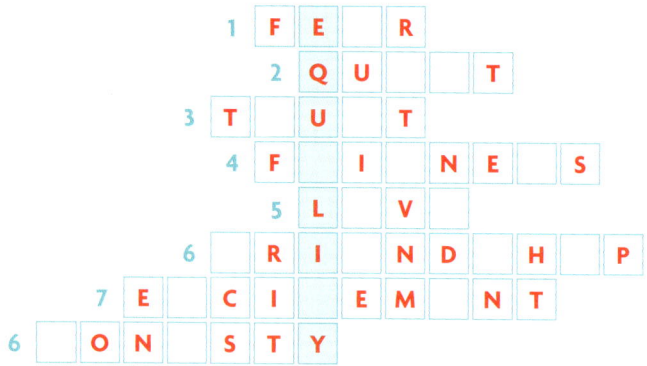

| **The text and beyond** • page 94
| **Values & Feelings** • page 110

The woman in the attic

One of the most memorable[1] characters in *Jane Eyre* is 'the mad woman in the attic', but we never hear her speak. Mr Rochester tells us something about her past life and her illness, but in many ways his wife remains a mystery. Perhaps it is not surprising, therefore, that many readers find that this mysterious woman lives on in the imagination. So is the 'woman in the attic' a bigger character in the story than we might think? These are some of themes in which the character of Bertha Mason helps us to understand the writing and the times of Charlotte Brontë.

Mental[2] illness in Victorian Britain

The Brontë family were fortunate to have a good library. Charlotte had access to many books, including books about medicine. These books show us that mental illness was of interest to doctors in Victorian Britain. A report from this time suggests in fact that people were starting to understand mental illness and mental health better than in previous times. For example doctors suggested that patients should have a view from a window and they should not be tied to furniture or locked in one room all the time.

---

1. **memorable** : something or someone you remember for a long time.
2. **mental** : the actions of the mind; how a person thinks, feels emotions, is conscious of actions, etc. E.g., mental illness is an illness of the mind; mental health shows us ways of having a healthy mind.

Even though doctors understood more about the needs of patients and wanted to show them some dignity,[3] asylums (hospitals for patients with mental illness) were still terrible places when compared to the modern day treatment of mental health. Many families chose to keep their relatives at home rather than send them to an asylum.

Interestingly, some historians have explored the connection between women expressing their feelings and madness[4] in Victorian Britain. In other words, a woman could be described as mad for being too 'emotional' or passionate. A husband only needed two doctors to agree that his wife was mad and he could take her to an asylum. It is said that the author Charles Dickens tried to put his wife in an asylum when she became angry about his mistress.

The role of women in the 19th century

For many centuries in Europe, women were thought to be less intelligent than men. Scientists even tried to show this was true by comparing how heavy their brains were! However, during the 19th century, the rights of women were often discussed in essays, novels and in politics. This led to changes later in the 19th and 20th century.

In the 19th century women were not allowed to vote.[5] Until 1870 their property belonged to their husband. Life for a middle-class Victorian woman centered around the home. Girls were taught how to be a good wife. A woman who wasn't married would still work caring for others, for example as a governess. Some women were not happy with this type of life. They wanted more independence. When Charlotte Brontë wrote *Jane Eyre*, some people thought that Jane was not a good role model for a female character. She was too passionate and independent. Bertha is also a strong character.

---

3. dignity : behaviour that brings or shows respect.
4. madness : the behaviour of someone who is mad (mentally ill).
5. vote : to indicate your preference by marking it on paper (here for a politician, leader, etc.).

Even though she is held in an attic, she is able to escape. She shows her passion and anger. Her husband cannot control her and people are afraid of her. In creating a woman who was mad and dangerous, Charlotte Brontë was able to give an unusual type of freedom to a female character.

Culture and identity[6]

Bertha is described as Creole (her mother is Caribbean and her father is British) and from a family of European settlers.[7] Many of these settlers went to make money from the sugar plantations[8] which were worked on by slaves.[9] In the 17th century, sugar was a luxury. However by the 19th century sugar was common everywhere. The plantations made a lot of money for the countries that had land on the islands. Some Caribbean islands later became part of the British Empire.

6. **identity** : the things that make a person or a group of people similar or different from each other.
7. **settlers** : Europeans who moved to countries in the 'new world', e.g. America, Caribbean, to start a new life.
8. **plantations** : large fields in hot countries for growing food or plants in big quantities.
9. **slaves** : people who are bought and sold; they work for the buyer or 'master'.

▶ *Slaves cutting the cane* (1823), from Ten Views in the Island of Antigua, by William Clark.

▶ *Wide Sargasso Sea* (1993), directed by John Duigan.

In 1833, Britain agreed to end slavery. This changed the lives of the families living on large plantations and some left. Many Europeans found themselves torn between two countries. They did not feel they belonged in England. In her novel *Wide Sargasso Sea* (1966), Jean Rhys writes about the difficulties of living between these two worlds. In *Wide Sargasso Sea*, Antoinette (Bertha) tells the story of her life in the Caribbean before and after she meets Mr Rochester. Later she is taken to England and we see some of the same events of *Jane Eyre*. In this way, we see life from the point of view of someone who has grown up with many different cultures and does not feel that they belong to one culture or identity. This was an experience for many people living and working in the British Empire.

The two Mrs Rochesters: the double in gothic fiction

Gothic fiction began in the 18th century and it was still popular the 19th century. Gothic novels try to create mystery and fear. Gothic novels often have 'doubles'. Doubles can be monsters or characters that show the fears and darker side of the main character or even fears about the future. In *Dr Jekyll and Mr Hyde* the 'double' is the same person. In *Frankenstein*, Victor Frankenstein comes to fear the monster (the creature) that he creates himself.

Although *Jane Eyre* is not a gothic novel, there are some gothic themes. Charlotte Brontë almost certainly read gothic novels and she liked creating fantasy worlds. At first Jane and Bertha seem very different, but if we look carefully, there are similarities. After all, they both marry Mr Rochester! Perhaps Mrs Rochester is Jane's double.

1 Comprehension Check • Are the following sentences true (T) or false (F). Correct the false ones.

		T	F
1.	Victorian doctors did not have any interest in mental health.	☐	☐
2.	A woman could be described as mad for being too passionate.	☐	☐
3.	A woman's duty was to look after the home and her family.	☐	☐
4.	European settlers went to the Caribbean to make money from the sugar plantations.	☐	☐
5.	*Wide Sargasso Sea* tells the story of Mr Mason and his friendship with Mr Rochester.	☐	☐
6.	Jane and Bertha are too different to be called 'doubles'.	☐	☐

2 Speaking • A question people ask about Mr Rochester's wife is: was she always mad or did she become mad? Discuss the questions.

1. Did Mr Rochester follow the advice of doctors at the time?
2. Do you think Mr Rochester did the right thing? Were there other options?
3. Bertha is taken to another country and locked in the attic. Mr Rochester says she was always 'mad' because of her family. Do you think this is true? Are there other explanations?

3 Writing • Write a short story from the viewpoint of a woman in the 19th century who is locked in a room but escapes at night. What do you see when you escape at night? Describe the house and the people in it.

Locations[1] *in* Jane Eyre

Settings are very important in Charlotte Brontë's *Jane Eyre*. As Jane Eyre grows up, we follow the journey of her life and her story through the places she lives. Even the names of the places like 'Thornfield' have hidden meanings. (In a rose, the part of the flower called a 'thorn' can cut.)

In writing the novel, Charlotte Brontë chose settings she knew. Although the places in *Jane Eyre* have fictional names (they are not real places) the settings for the story are mostly in the North of England where Charlotte lived. Some locations, like the home of the Reed family, were places she visited with her old school friend. Others, like the setting for Lowood School, were taken from Charlotte's own life. While the many film and televisions versions

1. **locations :** places (here places used for film and television or ideas for a story).

▶ View of Haddon Hall.

have used dramatic[2] locations like the Peak District in Derbyshire and historic country estates.

These are some of the incredible locations that have inspired[3] the telling of the story of Jane Eyre.

Gateshead

The first house that Jane lives in is her Aunt Reed's house called Gateshead. In 1839 Charlotte moved to Stone Gappe Hall to become a governess to the Sidgwick family. The house in Lothersdale, in North Yorkshire, was built in 1725 and is a fine old English hall. Although the reasons are not clear, Charlotte did not appear to have been happy there because she left the position shortly after she started.

In 2006, a TV series of *Jane Eyre* used the impressive Belton House in Lincolnshire in the East of England for Gateshead. Belton House is described as 'the perfect English country house'. The house is very big and has large gardens and an art collection. There are events and exhibitions at the house throughout the year.

Cowan Bridge School

At the age of eight, Charlotte and her sisters went to Cowan Bridge School near Kirby Lonsdale in Lancashire. Cowan Bridge was a school for the daughters of clergymen, like the Brontës. It was also a 'charity' school, or a school people gave money to for children who could not afford to pay for school. We know that Charlotte used Cowan Bridge as the idea for Lowood School because after *Jane Eyre* was published, the headmaster of the school wrote angry letters to Charlotte saying that her description of the school was not fair. Today, the site of the school is a collection of cottages in the village of the same name.

---

2. dramatic : full of action and excitement.
3. inspired : gave the ideas for (e.g. a book, a film, etc.).

In the 2011 film version of *Jane Eyre* directed by Cary Fukunaga, the location moves to the South of England to Broughton Castle. Broughton Castle dates back to the 14th century and has a moat.[4] It is open to visitors and can be used for events, too. But if a great house is not quite as people imagined the gloomy Lowood School, then perhaps the 17th century Gothic Ilam Hall is one of the more interesting locations. The hall is a Youth Hostel with real life dormitories.[5]

North Lees Hall

The home of Mr Rochester, the most famous location in *Jane Eyre* has to be Thornfield Hall. The location of Charlotte Brontë's imagination, however, has a direct connection to the story. Charlotte visited North Lees Hall two or three times while she was staying with her friend Ellen Nussey. Visitors to North Lees were even told stories of a mad woman who died in a fire there so it is not surprising that many people believe it is the inspiration for Thornfield Hall.

Film and television locations for Thornfield include large country estates like Haddon Hall, Renishaw Hall and Deene Park. Haddon Hall is a romantic, medieval hall in Bakewell in the North of England. The hall has appeared in over thirty different film locations, including three versions of *Jane Eyre*. As with all great historic halls, it has its own secret locations and the house even has a hidden door. The films by Cary Fukunaga and Franco Zeffirelli also use the impressive ruins of Wingfield Manor as the view for Thornfield Hall after the fire.

---

4. moat : a hole around a castle filled with water to stop it being attacked.
5. dormitories : large bedrooms with lots of beds.

Morton

The beautiful Peak District National Park has been used in almost all the versions of *Jane Eyre*. In the village of Hathersage, visitors can go for a walk around the locations and even find names from *Jane Eyre*. In 1845, Charlotte stayed for a while in Hathersage. The George Inn (now the George Hotel) was the village inn and the innkeeper of the time was called Mr Morton. Charlotte used the name Morton for the village where Jane lives with the Rivers family after she leaves Thornfield Hall.

The Peak District is an area of hills and open countryside of great natural beauty in the North of England. As well an as its grand country houses and dramatic scenery, the Peak District offers activities for walkers, cyclists and tourists of all ages.

1 Comprehension Check • Answer the following questions.

1. Are the places in *Jane Eyre* real places?
2. Where are most of the settings for *Jane Eyre*?
3. What did Charlotte do at Stone Gappe Hall?
4. How is Belton House described?
5. Which school did Charlotte use as the idea for Lowood School?
6. Who lived at North Lees Hall?
7. Name at least two film locations for Thornfield Hall.
8. Who was Mr Morton? Which place does Charlotte Brontë use the name of Morton for?

2 Writing • Imagine you want to plan a trip to one of the locations. Follow the instructions. This can also be a group activity.

Use a website to find out how to get to the location. Write the details in an email to a friend who is coming with you.
Prepare some questions for your tour guide. Is there anything you are curious about? Would you like to see any particular rooms or places from the story?

Cinema

- Title: *Jane Eyre*
- Year: 2011
- Director: Cary Fukunaga
- Starring: Mia Wasikowska; Michael Fassbender; Jamie Bell; Judi Dench.
- Location: UK

In this fascinating adaptation, directed by Cary Fukunaga, we follow Jane's journey to the Rivers' house, and her return to Thornfield and Mr Rochester. While she is with the Rivers, Jane remembers her childhood and the life she has left behind. Little by little she becomes stronger, not only in health, but emotionally as well, as she starts to understand her past, her present and her future.

1 Look at the poster of the film and answer the questions.

   1 Describe Jane. Is she how you imagine her?
   2 Whose face can you see in the poster?
   3 Do you think he is real or a memory?

2 Look at this still from the film and answer the questions.

   1 Describe where Jane is standing.
   2 Write a caption for what she is thinking.
   3 What will she do next?
   4 Imagine you could start the film at any time in the story. When would you begin Jane's story?

Activities

78 ▸ **The text and beyond**

Chapter 1	78
Chapter 2	80
Chapter 3	82
Chapter 4	84
Chapter 5	86
Chapter 6	88
Chapter 7	90
Chapter 8	92
Chapter 9	94

96 **Extensive listening**

98 **Surf the net**

100 **Trinity** • Preparation

102 **Preliminary** • Preparation

107 **Exit test** • Let's revise the story

110 **Values & Feelings**

Chapter 1

THE TEXT AND BEYOND

1 Comprehension Check • Complete the questions 1-6 with a word from the box. Then match and complete the answers a-f.

library   servants   promise   doctor   bedroom   house

1. ☐ What did Mr Reed ask Mrs Reed to .... she would do?
2. ☐ Why did John Reed try to hurt Jane in the .... ?
3. ☐ Why did Mrs Reed ask the .... to take Jane to the red room?
4. ☐ Why did no one ever go into the .... Jane was sent to that night?
5. ☐ Where did the .... suggest Jane go?
6. ☐ Was Jane sorry to leave Mrs Reed's .... ?

a   She thought Jane had tried to hurt ...
b   No, she only missed Bessie, the younger ...
c   Mrs Reed's husband had ...
d   He was cruel and wanted to punish her for taking a ....
e   To look after Jane Eyre as one of her own ...
f   He thought she might prefer to go to ...

Used to

I *used to* like looking at the pictures in the big books.

Used to + verb in the base form describes:
- A state or habit in the past.
- Actions that happened more than once.
- Actions that are now finished/complete.
- A past state with a present state, for example: *I used to live with my aunt when I was younger; I don't live there now.*

2 Grammar • Imagine Jane describing her life when she was younger to a new friend. Complete the sentences with the correct pronoun + '*used to*' + the verb in brackets in the infinitive as in the example.

Jane: Where did (play)? / *Where did you used to play?*

Friend: Where did (live) before you came to Lowood School? / *Where did you used to live?*

Jane: (live) at my aunt's house. / *I used to live at my aunt's house.*

Friend: Who did you live with?

Jane: My cousins. But, they were horrible. (tease) me.

Friend: Why? Didn't your aunt stop them?

Jane: No, (take) their side. She didn't really want me to live there.

Friend: She doesn't sound like a very nice lady.

Jane: She wasn't kind to me. (punish) me. Once she locked me in a cold, dark room.

Friend: You must be happy that you don't live there now.

Jane: Yes, but I miss Bessie. (tell) me stories.

3 Writing • Write six sentences about things you used to do that you don't do now.

4 Writing • Imagine you are Jane. Describe your experience in the "red room" in more detail. For example: what does the room look like; did you see a ghost – what did it look like?

5 Fill in the gaps • Read the notes from the doctor after his meeting with Jane. Complete the gaps with the best word.

I was called to see the patient after **(1)** .... fell. When I arrived the servants **(2)** .... put her in her own bed. **(3)** .... was blood on the cut at the side of the head. The patient looked pale **(4)** .... upset. I asked her **(5)** .... her fall. She told **(6)** .... that she was knocked down. I asked her about her life in the house. She should stay **(7)** .... bed for two **(8)** .... days.

Chapter 2

THE TEXT AND BEYOND

1 Comprehension Check • **Read the questions and choose the best answer — a, b or c.**

1. Did Jane feel happy when she arrived at Lowood School?
   a ☐ No, she was sad that she had left Mrs Reed's house.
   b ☐ Yes, she was excited to start her new lessons.
   c ☐ No, she found the school cold and forbidding.

2. Did Jane like her teachers?
   a ☐ No, she found all of them strict and unfriendly.
   b ☐ She didn't like them very much but Miss Temple was kind.
   c ☐ She neither liked or disliked her teachers.

3. What did Helen tell Jane about Mr Brocklehurst?
   a ☐ He owned the school but he was not a generous man.
   b ☐ He was a kind man who bought all their food and clothes.
   c ☐ He thought that only strong girls should continue studying.

4. What happened in the spring?
   a ☐ Many of the girls died of an infectious disease.
   b ☐ Helen looked after Jane who had become ill.
   c ☐ The weather was very cold so the girls became ill.

5. What did Helen mean when she said 'goodbye'?
   a ☐ She was going to leave the school and not return.
   b ☐ She wanted to let Jane know she was dying.
   c ☐ She was going to travel somewhere far away.

6. Did things change at Lowood school?
   a ☐ Some things changed but the food was still terrible.
   b ☐ The conditions weren't always healthy, but the girls were happier.
   c ☐ Conditions at the school improved after an inquiry.

2 Vocabulary • Match the words to the descriptions.

a classroom **b** pupils **c** head teacher **d** exam **e** subject **f** homework

1. ☐ This person has a responsibility to look after the school and its students.
2. ☐ A test to see how well you understand the things you have been learning.
3. ☐ Something you study in lessons at school.
4. ☐ A place where students have lessons.
5. ☐ Work to do at home or after class.
6. ☐ Another name for students in a school.

3 Reading • Read the text about charity schools in Victorian England. Put the paragraphs a-d in chronological order (in the order the events happen).

a ☐ Although rich men and women gave money (charity) to these schools, it was not until later in the 1800s that the government began to look at the conditions. Before this time, there were no national organisations or rules about how the children should be looked after or taught.

b ☐ Before the 19th century, education in schools was mostly for rich families who could afford to pay the fees. Education for girls was not common and there were only a few schools for girls. Poorer children received very little, if any, education.

c ☐ Around 1870, the money for non-private schools no longer came from wealthy individuals. It was paid for by cities or towns. This was the beginning of the modern education system in England. By the end of the 19th century all children had to go to school until they were 12 years old and education was free.

d ☐ Then, around the early 1800s, the Church began 'charity schools' to give poorer children a basic education, such as reading, writing and studying the bible. Girls from middle-class families might learn subjects that were useful as a wife or a governess. The schools were often very strict.

4 Speaking • If you were going to improve your school in your country, what things would you like to improve? Practice using '*I would ....*' and '*should*'.

Chapter 3

THE TEXT AND BEYOND

1 Comprehension Check • Choose the best word to complete the sentences about Chapter Three. Then put the sentences in order to make a summary of Chapter Three.

- **a** ☐ One winter Jane helped *an interesting / a stupid* stranger who had fallen from his horse.
- **b** ☐ Jane thought Mr Rochester might *marry / congratulate* Blanche Ingram.
- **c** ☐ Jane stayed for eight more *months / years* at Lowood and became a teacher there.
- **d** ☐ Mr Rochester returned one day with some *visitors / cousins*.
- **e** ☐ Jane woke up in the middle of the night after hearing a terrible *cry / laugh*.
- **f** ☐ She looked for a job and became a *teacher / governess* at Thornfield Hall.
- **g** ☐ Although Jane found Mr Rochester *frightening / rude* at first, she started to like his company.
- **h** ☐ There was *a fire / water* in Mr Rochester's bedroom and Jane helped to put it out.

2 Comprehension Check • Look at Chapter Three again. Find sentences that describe:

1. A quiet life.
2. Exciting or frightening events.

3 Game • Use the word squares to move across the grid. The words can have either similar or opposite meanings. You can go up, down or across but the squares must be next to each other. There is more than one way across.

4 Characters • Which character changes Jane's life from quiet to exciting or different? Use two or three adjectives (or phrases) from Chapter Three to describe:

1. Mrs Fairfax ....
2. Adèle ....
3. Mr Rochester ....
4. Blanche Ingram ....

5 Fill in the gaps • Complete the advert Jane places in the newspaper with the words form the word pool.

> salary   governess   piano   teacher   write   pupil   paint   French

Position wanted

I am a **(1)** .... at Lowood School, where I was also a **(2)** .... for six years. I am looking for a position as a **(3)** .... in a family for at least 12 months. I can read and **(4)** .... English to a good standard. I can speak **(5)** ...., I can **(6)** .... and draw, and I can play the **(7)** ....
I am able to start immediately. My present **(8)** .... is 15 pounds a month.

Miss Jane Eyre

6 Writing • Imagine you are Mrs Fairfax. Write a response to the advert. You should:

- say you would like Jane to start work
- tell her what her duties will be
- tell her how much she will be paid and any benefits, e.g. food and accommodation
- suggest a date for her to start and any other details, e.g. travel arrangements
- say how she should reply if she wants to accept the position

Chapter 4

THE TEXT AND BEYOND

1 Comprehension Check • **Are the following sentences true (T) or false (F)? Correct the false ones.**

		T	F
1.	If Mr Rochester married Blanche Ingram he might send Adèle to school.	☐	☐
2.	Mr Rochester was very happy to see Mr Mason.	☐	☐
3.	The guests came out of their rooms because they heard a loud scream.	☐	☐
4.	Mr Rochester told the visitors to return to their rooms.	☐	☐
5.	Jane stayed with Mr Mason for a while because he was angry.	☐	☐
6.	Another friend came to see Mr Mason.	☐	☐
7.	Mr Rochester asks Jane to come and sit with him in the library.	☐	☐
8.	Mr Rochester was afraid of what Mr Mason might say.	☐	☐

2 Speaking • **Use the following images to describe the main events in Chapter Four.**

3 Vocabulary • **In Chapter Four, the guests play a game called 'charades'. Choose a word from Chapter Four. Can the other persons or team guess which word you are acting out?**

4 Writing • **Imagine you are one of the guests. You do not trust Mr Rochester's story. You want to find out more. Write some questions for each situation. Practice responding to the questions with another student.**

- You see another guest at breakfast. Ask them what they heard and what they think it was.
- You ask one of the servants about the events. Remember your position. Try not to sound too interested.
- You see Mr Rochester again. What do you ask him? What about his friend from the West Indies?

5 Interpretation • **Life is quite confusing for Jane in Chapter Four. Think about the situations (1-3). What would you do?**

1. Mr Rochester might marry Blanche Ingram.
   - **a** ☐ Look for another job, then you're prepared.
   - **b** ☐ Ask Mr Rochester not to marry this woman because she's proud.
   - **c** ☐ Tell Blanche that the house is haunted.
2. Mr Rochester asks you to look after Mr Mason.
   - **a** ☐ Ask him for more information about the noises you heard.
   - **b** ☐ Explore the attic when you are on your own.
   - **c** ☐ Do as he asks. He's your employer. You'll find out in time.
3. Mr Rochester tells you he is worried about what Mr Mason might do.
   - **a** ☐ Don't worry about it. It's not your problem.
   - **b** ☐ If he wants your help, he needs to tell you everything. Ask for an explanation.
   - **c** ☐ Try to find out more about Mr Mason but don't tell Mr Rochester.

6 Reading pictures • **Answer the following questions.**

1. Who are the people in the picture on page 29? What are they doing?
2. Who is coming down the stairs on page 30? What is he saying?
3. Who is in the picture on page 33? What is happening?

Chapter 5

THE TEXT AND BEYOND

1 Comprehension Check • **Read the first part of each sentence (1-6) and match it with a conclusion (a-h). There are two conclusions that you do not need to use.**

1. ☐ Even up until the moment of her death …
2. ☐ Jane was upset at the thought that …
3. ☐ Jane was surprised when Mr Rochester told her that …
4. ☐ A coachman who told Jane that her aunt was ill …
5. ☐ Mr Rochester told Jane that Adèle would go to school and …
6. ☐ Jane found out that she had an uncle but …

a   he wanted to marry her and not Miss Ingram.
b   was the husband of Mrs Reed's maid Bessie.
c   Mrs Reed had told him that Jane was dead.
d   Adèle was a good girl and wanted to go to school.
e   Mr Rochester might marry Miss Ingram.
f   she would not be able to remain as a governess.
g   Mrs Reed disliked Jane.
h   the news that her cousin John had died.

2 Characters • **Who do the sentences describe?**

1. She still disliked Jane even when she was dying. ……………………………………
2. She was rich and beautiful, but proud. ……………………………………
3. He had no children of his own and wanted to look after his niece. ……………
4. He didn't want to marry Miss Ingram. ……………………………………
5. She couldn't believe Mr Rochester's words. ……………………………………
6. He said Jane would need to leave but it wasn't true. ……………………………………

3 Writing • Who has written these letters? Choose one and write a reply.

1 Dear Mr Reed,

Thank you for your letter. I am sorry to have to tell you that your niece, Jane Eyre, died a few years ago at Lowood School of an infectious disease. My son John is looking for work. Do you require any assistants?

2 Dear Mrs Fairfax, please can you let Mr Rochester know that my aunt, Mrs Reed, is very unwell and I must stay here for a few more weeks. I will return to Thornfield as soon as I can.

Clauses of concession

Even though **I was surprised that my aunt wished to see me, I couldn't say no to this request.**

- A sentence or clause that begins with the words *although*, *even though* or *though* is called a **clause of concession**. They are all used in the same way. *Even though* is sometimes stronger and *though* can be a little less formal.
- *Although/even* and *though/though* are used to introduce an idea that is surprising or opposite to (contrasts with) the second part of the sentence. For example: **Although** Mrs Reed wanted me to visit her, she still hated me.

4 Grammar • Match the first part of the sentence (1-5) with a second part (a-f) to make logical sentences using '*although*'. There is more than one possibility.

(0) I had not seen him for a long time… (e) He still remembered me.
Although I had not seen him for a long time, he still remembered me.

0.	I had not seen him for a long time…	**a**	I knew I had to leave.
1.	He was sometimes rude to me in the past…	**b**	I liked his company and conversation.
2.	She is rich and beautiful…	**c**	I felt there was something wrong.
3.	I was happy…	**d**	He is gentle and kind with me now.
4.	I wanted to stay…	**e**	`0` He still remembered me.
5.	We had different opinions…	**f**	He doesn't want to marry her.

Chapter 6

THE TEXT AND BEYOND

1 Comprehension Check • Choose the best answer – a, b or c.

1. Why did Jane write to her uncle?
   a ☐ She wanted to tell him that she was getting married.
   b ☐ She wanted him to send her some money.
   c ☐ He knew Mr Rochester.

2. Who came to Jane's room before the wedding?
   a ☐ A lady who told her that she was Grace Poole.
   b ☐ A lady that she had never seen before.
   c ☐ A ghost in a long white dress holding a candle.

3. What happened when Jane woke up the next day?
   a ☐ She found her veil torn to pieces on the floor.
   b ☐ She understood that she had had a bad dream.
   c ☐ She ran to Mr Rochester and told him immediately.

4. Who arrived unexpectedly during the wedding ceremony?
   a ☐ The woman Jane had seen with her brother.
   b ☐ A clergyman and Mr Mason.
   c ☐ Mr Mason and a lawyer called Mr Briggs.

5. Why did they want to stop the marriage from happening?
   a ☐ Mr Mason's sister was angry about the wedding.
   b ☐ Mr Rochester was already married.
   c ☐ Mr Rochester did not really want to marry Jane.

6. Who was Bertha Mason?
   a ☐ Mr Rochester's cousin and a relative of Mr Mason.
   b ☐ A relation of Grace Poole who looked after her.
   c ☐ Mr Mason's sister and Mr Rochester's wife.

2 Speaking • Answer the following question.

Which marriage do you think the title refers to? What is the secret?

3 Fill in the gaps
• Complete the sentences with a word from the box. Which of these facts about marriage and divorce in Victorian England do you think are true? Check the answers at the bottom of the page.

> divorce   wife   husband   marry   widow   bigamist

1. ☐ It was legal to be a .... : to marry a second wife when still married.
2. ☐ In Victorian times .... was expensive and difficult.
3. ☐ Women were often taught how to be a good ....
4. ☐ It was common for women to .... late in life compared to today.
5. ☐ Even a wealthy .... received no money when her husband died.
6. ☐ Until 1870 a woman's property belonged to her .... after she married.

4 Reading pictures
• Look at the pictures on pages 42-43 and 45 and answer the questions.

1. Who is in the picture on pages 42-43?
2. What is she doing?
3. What is happening on page 45?

5 Writing
• Imagine you could write a speech or a thought bubble like a cartoon. Write words for each character in the church showing what they are either thinking or saying. Now create a thought bubble for Bertha, Mr Rochester's wife, when she finds the veil and when he comes to the attic after the wedding.

6 Speaking
• Discuss the following questions.

1. How do you think Mr Mason and the lawyer knew about the wedding?
2. Should Mr Rochester be allowed to divorce his wife?
3. Was Jane right to leave?
4. Do you think anybody has behaved badly? If so, who? Why?

Key: **1** bigamist - F (it was not legal); **2** divorce - T; **3** wife - T; **4** marry - F (the average age was 20-22 compared to 25-32 in the UK); **5** F (some widows did receive money from their husband's property); **6** T (1870 Married Woman's Property Act).

Chapter 7

THE TEXT AND BEYOND

1 Comprehension Check • Complete the sentences 1-8 with a question word from the word box and answer the questions. You can use each question word twice.

What   Where   Why   Who

1. .... did Jane leave in the coach?
2. .... did Jane see in the house?
3. .... did the servant give Jane?
4. .... did Jane stay the night?
5. .... did Jane not want to give her real name?
6. .... did Jane think St John was serious?
7. .... did Jane start work?
8. .... came to see Jane in the cottage?

2 Writing • You are a private investigator and you must find Jane. Write a report about where she went and what has happened. Remember – you can't go into the house. You can only watch from outside. Use the clues to help you.

Found: purse and a small suitcase. Please ask at the Coach Inn.

Services at St Marks / 10 am. St John Rivers Clergyman

Moreton Village School – Now taking pupils

Dear Doctor Daniel – the young woman who came to us is much better. Thanks for your kind advice. Diana Rivers

3 Game • **Complete the picture crossword with words from Chapter Seven.**

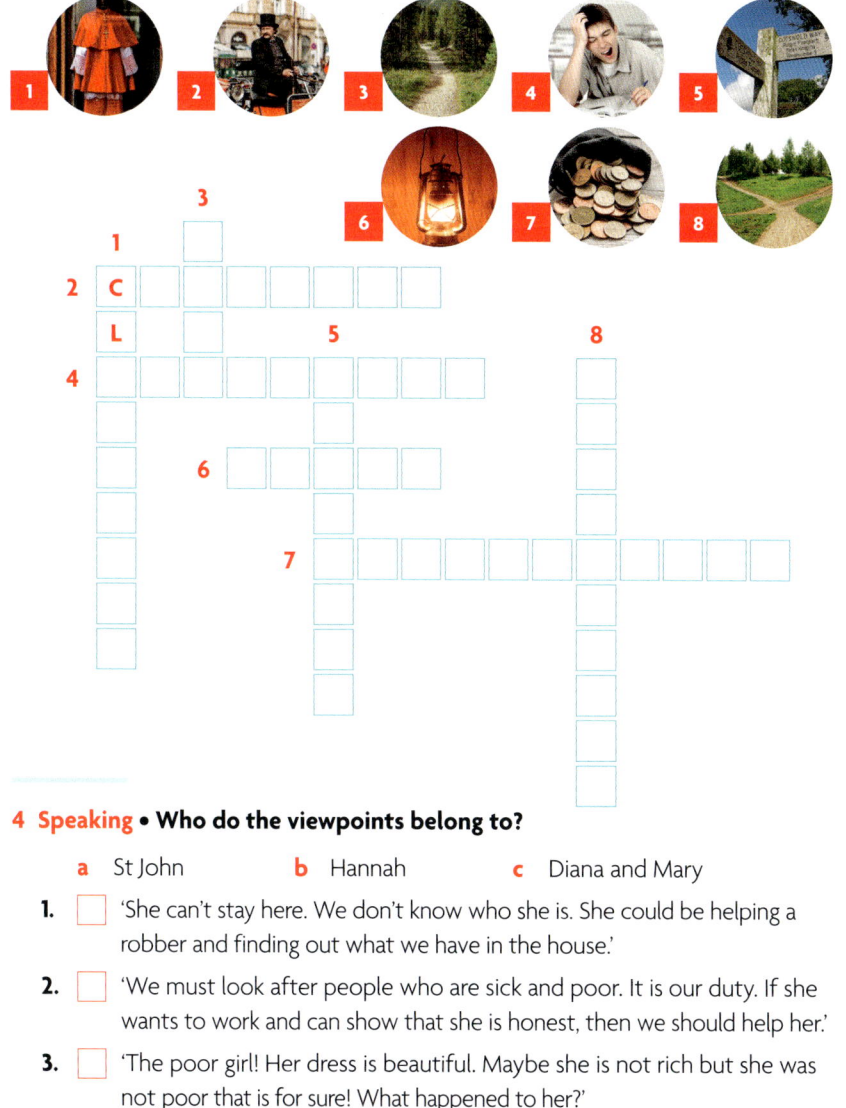

4 Speaking • **Who do the viewpoints belong to?**

    a St John   **b** Hannah   **c** Diana and Mary

1. ☐ 'She can't stay here. We don't know who she is. She could be helping a robber and finding out what we have in the house.'

2. ☐ 'We must look after people who are sick and poor. It is our duty. If she wants to work and can show that she is honest, then we should help her.'

3. ☐ 'The poor girl! Her dress is beautiful. Maybe she is not rich but she was not poor that is for sure! What happened to her?'

91

Chapter 8

THE TEXT AND BEYOND

1 Comprehension Check • **Complete sentences 1-8 with the missing words to make a summary of the story.**

paintings   school   voice   lawyer   uncle   wife   letter   Thornfield   money

1. The people of the village liked Jane and the ……………… was successful.
2. One evening St John tore a piece of paper from one of Jane's ……………… .
3. Later St John told Jane that he had received a letter from a ……………… called Mr Briggs.
4. He now knew everything about Jane's past. He told her she had inherited money from her ……………… .
5. Jane also found out St John and his sisters were her cousins and decided to share the ……………… with them.
6. Jane wrote a ……………… to Mrs Fairfax to ask about Mr Rochester but received no reply.
7. St John asked Jane to come to India with him as his ………………, but Jane did not love him.
8. Jane thought she heard a ……………… calling her. She left for ……………… the next day.

2 Vocabulary • **Complete the puzzle with words from exercise 1. Whose voice did Jane hear?**

92

3 Vocabulary • Find the word *supernatural* in a dictionary. Which words can be used to describe the supernatural? Use a dictionary, if necessary.

clear   strange   ghostly   unexplained   real   mysterious
scientific   believable   incredible   weird   eerie   obvious

4 Vocabulary • Which of these word pairs do you think are found in: a) realist novels; b) gothic novels?

strange feelings ☐   real settings ☐   remote locations ☐
mysterious events ☐   believable events ☐   logical explanation ☐

5 Fill in the gaps • Complete the text with words from exercise 4. Read and check.

Jane Eyre and the supernatural

Many people describe *Jane Eyre* as a realist novel. A realist novel has (**1**) .... settings with (**2**) .... events that the readers can understand and imagine for themselves. In other words, although incredible things happen, there is usually a reason for them. Readers the 19th century could imagine the people, houses, and the difficulties of an orphan and governess like Jane.

However, although there are many real events, there are some events that are more difficult to explain. We can describe these as the supernatural. These type of events are more common in gothic novels. Gothic novels use (**3**) .... locations and (**4**) .... events to create feelings of curiosity and fear.

One example of this is when Jane is deciding what to do about St John's proposal and she hears the Mr Rochester's voice. She has a (**5**) .... feeling that Mr Rochester is trying to tell her something without being there in person. This feeling is so strong that she must act on the voice she hears. Of course, there may be a logical (**6**) .... Or maybe it is just a mystery.

6 Speaking • Answer the following questions.

1. Do you believe in things that can't be explained?

2. Do you think that dreams or voices can tell us things?

3. Have you (or anyone you know) had a strange experience?

Chapter 9

THE TEXT AND BEYOND

1 Comprehension Check • Read the sentences and mark them (T) for true, (F) for false or (D) for doesn't say.

		T	F	D
1.	When Jane arrived at Thornfield, it was exactly the same.	☐	☐	☐
2.	Mr Rochester's wife started the fire.	☐	☐	☐
3.	Mr Rochester was injured in the fire.	☐	☐	☐
4.	The servants at Ferndean were sad for Mr Rochester.	☐	☐	☐
5.	Mr Rochester told Jane to go away when she first arrived.	☐	☐	☐
6.	Jane and Mr Rochester were married.	☐	☐	☐
7.	Adèle married a clergyman.	☐	☐	☐
8.	Sadly Mr Rochester was never able to see again.	☐	☐	☐

2 Comprehension Check • In Chapter Nine, Jane says the words 'Reader, I married him'. What do these words tell us about Jane? There is more than one possibility.

1. Jane really wants to get married and in the end she finds a husband.
2. Jane is an independent woman who can decide who she marries.
3. Jane's love for Mr Rochester is everything. No one else matters.

3 Speaking • Imagine you were there at the time of the fire. You are interviewed by the newspaper. Answer the questions. Practice with another student and make some questions of your own.

1. What happened?
2. Who started the fire?
3. Did anyone die or get injured?

4 Writing • Use the interview in exercise 3 to write a newspaper story about the fire.

Example: An eye witness said that Mrs Rochester had escaped. / Mr Rochester's servant said that Mrs Rochester had started the fire.

Past Perfect

Little Adèle came back to live with us when she *had finished* school.

Event 1
Adèle finishes school.

Event 2
Adèle goes to live with Jane and Mr Rochester.

Look at the example. What tense do we use for the event happens first?

When telling a story in the past simple, the **Past Perfect Simple** is used for the event that happened before the event in the past simple.

5 Grammar • Rewrite the sentences about Chapter Nine using the correct tense and the connecting word in brackets. There is an example at the beginning (0).

0. Jane [return] to Thornfield a year/she [left]. (after)
   Jane returned to Thornfield a year after she had left.
1. At first everything [seem] the same/Jane [left] it. (as)
2. When Jane arrived she [see]/the house [burn] down. (that)
3. She [go] to the village to ask/[happen] to the house. (what)
4. Mr Rochester [try] to save his wife/she already [jump] from the roof. (but)
5. Jane [go] to see Mr Rochester/she [visit] the inn. (after)
6. She [see]/Mr Rochester [lose] a hand in the fire. (that)

6 Vocabulary • Which of these adjectives describes a hero? Use a dictionary to find new words.

| mad | brave | afraid | mischievous | rebellious | courageous | cruel | nasty |
| epic | generous | good | famous | noble | shy | moody | bad | romantic |

7 Writing • Make a list of heroes in films or books. Then answer the questions.

1. Which heroes have superpowers or are like gods?
2. Which heroes have secrets or do bad things as well?
3. Is it possible to be a hero and a villain?
4. Describe Mr Rochester. Why do you think Jane loves him?

EXTENSIVE LISTENING

1 Extensive listening • **Listen to the conversations. Put a tick in the box below the correct picture.**

1. Which subject do Charlotte and Sue's daughter Emily both like?

  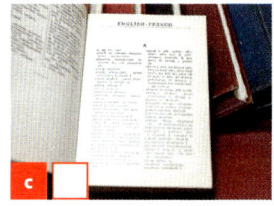

2. What does the housekeeper ask the maid to put in the room of the bride and bridegroom?

3. How much will Amer spend to go to his cousin's house?

4. Which type of house does Jane want to live in?

2 Extensive listening • Listen to the job interview and complete the candidate notes.

track 12

Name of the candidate: **(0)** *Jane Elliott*

Education: Leeds **(1)** .... Degree in **(2)** .... (Primary school). Subject: **(3)** .... Previous experience: Rivers Primary School (from age **(4)** ....); Thornfield School for **(5)** .... (age 10 to 11). Job as a teaching **(6)** .... at Lowood Primary School. Worked in Spain during the **(7)** .... holidays in an activity club. (Activities included: **(8)** ...., painting and organising **(9)** ....).

Additional information (interests, etc.): **(10)** .... animals from **(11)** .... (origami); likes making **(12)** ....

3 Extensive listening • Listen to the news report about a fire. Read the statements. Answer true (T) or false (F).

track 13

		T	F
1.	The fire took place late at night.	☐	☐
2.	Police do not yet know how the fire started.	☐	☐
3.	The fire brigade rescued the woman on the roof quickly.	☐	☐
4.	Residents can return home tomorrow.	☐	☐
5.	Some of the residents are staying in hotels.	☐	☐

4 Extensive listening • You will hear four people talking about marriage and relationships. Write the number of the speaker (1-4) next to a summary of what they say. There is one sentence you will not need.

track 14

a. ☐ This person has everything planned. They just need to find someone to marry!

b. ☐ This person thinks that people shouldn't get married because there are too many divorces.

c. ☐ This person does not believe you have to marry for love to have a successful marriage.

d. ☐ This person does not think that they are ready to get married just yet.

e. ☐ This person believes you know almost immediately if someone is the right person.

SURF THE NET

Haworth and the Brontë family

Haworth is a pretty village in the North of England, in the county of Yorkshire. Haworth is famous for its connection to the Brontë family. The Brontë sisters wrote many of their famous works while living there.

Use an Internet search engine to find out more about Haworth and the Brontë family.

1. Where is the museum?
2. What is it called?
3. What else can you do at the museum?
4. Why is the Old School Room of interest?
5. Can you find any pictures of the Brontë family?
6. Can you find any events in Haworth or 'Brontë Country'?
7. Has Haworth appeared in any films?
8. Find at least three more interesting facts about the area or the Brontë family.

Daily life in Victorian Britain

There were many changes during the Victorian Age for people of all social levels. The changes happened very quickly. There were more and more factories and big developments in science, travel and technology.

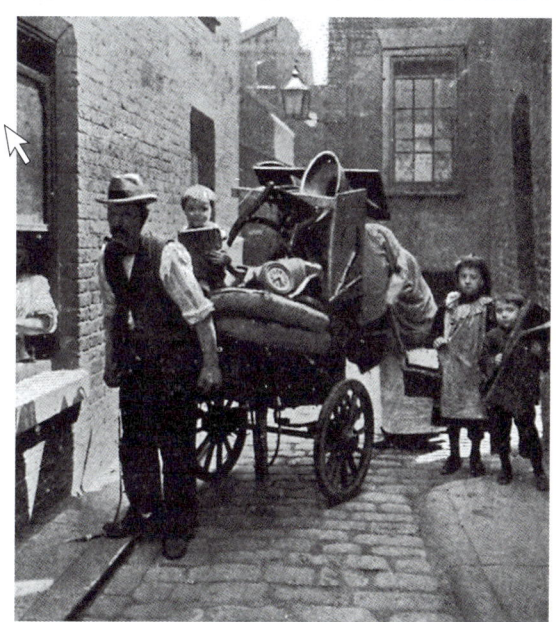

Use an Internet search engine to find out more about daily life in Victorian Britain.

1. Describe at least three things that changed people's lives during the time that Queen Victoria was queen.
2. Describe life for:
   a very rich people;
   b middle class people;
   c workers and the very poor.
3. Describe the different types of houses.
4. Did all children go to school?
5. What did Victorian families do for entertainment?

TRINITY • Preparation

1 GESE GRADE 6 – Health and fitness • Match the symptoms to the cause and answer the questions.

a headache   b stomach ache   c cold   d flu

1. ☐ My muscles are aching and I'm hot and cold.
2. ☐ I feel sick and I don't want to eat anything.
3. ☐ My head hurts and I can't concentrate.
4. ☐ I have a bad cough and I have a sore throat.

- Have you ever been ill?
- What medicine did you need to take?
- If you don't eat healthy food, what might happen?

2 GESE GRADE 6 – Rules and regulations • Read the rules and regulations for Lowood School. Use them to help you discuss the questions about rules and regulations using the phrases in italics.

Pupils *are not allowed* more than 2 pieces of bread each day.
If a girl is disobedient, she *won't* be given any supper.
Girls *must* keep their uniforms clean and tidy.
All pupils *have to* wash their hands. Cold water is not an excuse!

1. What are you *allowed / not allowed* to do at your *school / college / place of work*?
2. If you don't follow the rules, what will happen?
3. Are there any rules you must follow that you disagree with? Give examples. Say why.
4. Were rules stricter in the past than they are now? (*You couldn't / were not allowed to...*)

3 GESE GRADE 6 – Learning a foreign language • **Jane learns French. Adèle is French, so she must learn English. Complete the sentences about learning a foreign language. Ask another person questions about this topic using the following sentences to help you start the discussion.**

1. How do you prefer to .... a foreign language?
2. Have you ever .... to a country where you don't speak the language?
3. What .... the disadvantages, if you don't learn another language?
4. Is it better to learn a language in the .... the language is spoken, or in your own country?
5. Is it easier to learn with someone who .... your language, or someone who doesn't?

4 GESE GRADE 6 – Travel • **Use the photos to describe how Jane travels in *Jane Eyre*. Were there any other ways a person could travel in the mid-1800s? Discuss the questions about travel.**

1. Why do people travel?
2. Is it quicker to travel today? Give examples.
3. What is the furthest distance you have ever walked? Have you ever been on a walking holiday?
4. Are you travelling anywhere this summer/winter? Describe your plans.

PRELIMINARY • Preparation

CHAPTERS 1-3

1 Reading Part 1 • Look at the text in each question. What does it say?

0
John Reed Library
Quiet Zone
Users are reminded to turn off mobile phones

a ☐ You can't talk here but you may use your phone.
b ✔ You must turn your phone off in this area.
c ☐ There is only one quiet zone in the library.

1
National Coach Lines Bradford to Gateshead
Journey time: 3 hours
Single £12/Return £20

a ☐ It costs £12 for a 3 hour journey.
b ☐ National Coach Lines' head office is in Bradford.
c ☐ It costs less to travel to Gateshead than Bradford.

2
Great value on school uniforms
Sale ends on 31st August.
It's cool to go back to school!

a ☐ The shop only sells uniforms in August.
b ☐ The uniforms are poor quality.
c ☐ Uniforms are reduced until the end of August.

3
Hello everyone,
Just a reminder that there are no English classes during the exam period from 1st – 14th July.

Sue Brown
Schools Administrator

a ☐ There are not going to be any more classes.
b ☐ There are no English classes when there are exams.
c ☐ Sue Brown is the English teacher.

2 Writing Part 2 • Your friend, Samira, has invited you to come and stay with her at her auntie's house in the countryside. Write an email to Samira. In your email, you should:

- accept the invitation;
- tell her you're excited and ask about the house;
- ask how you are going to go/travel there;
- ask her what you need to bring with you.

Write your email in about 35-45 words.

3 Speaking Part 3 • The photographs show people learning at school and at home. Work with a partner to describe the photographs.

4 Speaking Part 4 • Talk together different ways to learn. You can use the suggestions to help you.

1. Talk about the advantages of studying at home and at school.
2. Talk about studying on your own and with others.
3. Talk about how things have changed from the past to now.
4. Talk about studying online.

PRELIMINARY • Preparation

CHAPTERS 4-6

5 Reading Part 5 • Read the text below and choose the correct word for each space. For each question, mark the correct letter a, b, c, or d.

Entertaining in the great country (**0**) ..*houses*.. of England was part of a social tradition. People from high society (**1**) .... such events to make business arrangements or deals, meet new people and find husbands or wives. In the 18th and 19th century (**2**) .... to country houses often stayed for (**3**) .... days and sometimes weeks. One reason for this was the difficulty (**4**) .... travelling long distances and the poor quality of the roads. However, often, the hosts had long parties (**5**) .... they wanted to show their wealth and power through (**6**) .... generosity and ability to entertain. The longer they could entertain for, the wealthier they were. A good host or hostess would plan activities for his or her guests (**7**) .... day. These might include both outdoor walks and sport, (**8**) .... shooting, and indoor games like charades. Food was (**9**) .... important part of the house party and a good housekeeper knew how to prepare the best recipes for such visits. During the 1800s, the Country House party was so popular that books were even (**10**) .... on the subject.

0.	**a** houses	**b**	homes	**c**	villages	**d**	cottages
1.	**a** use	**b**	used	**c**	made	**d**	done
2.	**a** visitors	**b**	guest	**c**	ladies	**d**	tourists
3.	**a** number	**b**	few	**c**	several	**d**	much
4.	**a** for	**b**	by	**c**	to	**d**	of
5.	**a** because	**b**	why	**c**	before	**d**	by
6.	**a** their	**b**	her	**c**	him	**d**	them
7.	**a** any	**b**	for	**c**	a	**d**	each
8.	**a** as	**b**	like	**c**	only	**d**	when
9.	**a** then	**b**	never	**c**	another	**d**	too
10.	**a** written	**b**	writes	**c**	write	**d**	writing

6 Writing Part 3 • Your English teacher has asked you to write a story. Your story must begin with this sentence: One day I heard a terrible scream...

Write your answer in about 100 words.

CHAPTERS 7-9

7 Reading Part 3 • **Look at the sentences below about missionaries in the Victorian Age. Read the text and decide if each sentence is correct or incorrect. If it is correct, mark A. If it is incorrect, mark B.**

Missionaries in the Victorian Age

Missionaries were men or women who travelled to foreign countries to teach their religion to the people who lived there. Missionaries often learnt local languages and travelled to remote, isolated places. In Charlotte Brontë's *Jane Eyre*, St John Rivers wants to become a missionary. He tries to teach Jane the languages of Sanskrit and Hindustani, to prepare for the life he imagined in British India.

The Victorian Age was a time of social change and questioning of ideals, philosophy and faith. The missionaries wanted to share their ideas about society as well as their beliefs. In some cases they tried to change the economic and social conditions. Missionaries did not only travel to foreign countries. They worked in Britain, too, and they had their own newspapers and publications.

Travel to new countries could be dangerous for both the missionaries and the people they went to live with. The missionaries were not always used to the conditions they were living in and many died. However, the local inhabitants could also catch new infectious diseases from the missionaries.

Famous missionaries of the age include David Livingstone who went to Africa as a missionary doctor and William Carey who translated the Bible into Bengali, Hindi and many other languages.

	A	B
11. The main reason missionaries went abroad was to teach English.	☐	☐
12. In *Jane Eyre*, St John Rivers imagines a life as a missionary.	☐	☐
13. The Victorian Age was not a time of change.	☐	☐
14. Missionaries only shared their faith with each other.	☐	☐
15. It was sometimes quite dangerous to be a missionary.	☐	☐
16. The people in the countries the missionaries travelled to did not get diseases.	☐	☐
17. David Livingstone was a doctor as well as a famous missionary.	☐	☐
18. William Carey was a famous Victorian missionary and translator.	☐	☐

8 Writing Part 3 • **This is part of an email. Reply to the person, giving some advice.**

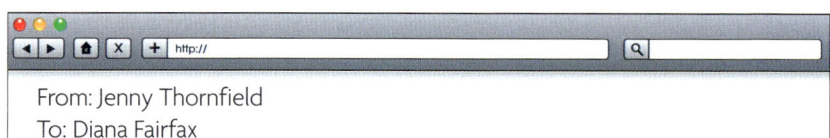

From: Jenny Thornfield
To: Diana Fairfax

Hi Diana! How are you? How's your brother?

Well, I should start by telling you our exciting news. Scott has asked me to marry him, and I said... yes!

It was such a surprise that I haven't thought about the wedding yet, but I need your help. You are a lot better at organising things! Do you know of any good places to get married? Do you think it's better to go abroad? I'd like to book the same place for everything: the wedding ceremony, the meal, the evening entertainment. What do you think?

9 Speaking Part 2 • **A man is going to work in a small village in India. The village is isolated but he will sometimes be able to connect to the Internet. Talk with a classmate about how he should prepare. Here are some pictures with some ideas to help you.**

LET'S REVISE THE STORY

1 Picture summary • The following pictures are not in the right order. Put them in the order they appear in the book and write a short summary under each one to say what's happening.

a

....
....

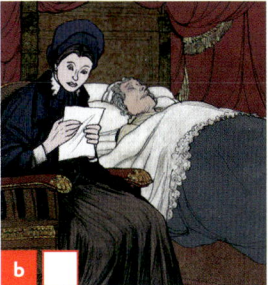

b

....
....

c

....
....

d

....
....

e

....
....

f

....
....

g

....
....

h

....
....

i

....
....

LET'S REVISE THE STORY

2 Comprehension • **Complete the questions about the story with a question word (*who*, *what*, *when*, *where*, *why*) and match each question to an answer.**

0. What happened when Jane was in the Red Room? / g. She became very scared and she fainted.
1. .... did some girls die at Lowood School?
2. .... was Miss Temple?
3. .... did Mr Mason first arrive at Thornfield?
4. .... did Mrs Reed tell Jane's Uncle in Madeira?
5. .... was Jane surprised when Mr Rochester proposed?
6. .... did someone come into Jane's room?
7. .... lived in the attic?
8. .... did Jane go when she left Thornfield Hall?
9. .... did Jane not want to marry St John?
10. .... did Jane go when she saw Thornfield had burnt down?
11. .... happened at the end of the story?

a ☐ To a house in a small village where some kind people let her in.
b ☐ She did not think that he loved her and she did not love him.
c ☐ She went to find Mr Rochester at Ferndean.
d ☐ Mr Rochester's wife with her nurse Grace Poole.
e ☐ When Mr Rochester had visitors at the house.
f ☐ Mr Rochester and Jane got married and had children.
g ☐ 0 ☐ She became very scared and she fainted.
h ☐ She said that Jane had died at Lowood School.
i ☐ Two nights before her wedding day.
j ☐ She was his governess and she thought he wanted to marry Blanche.
k ☐ The headmistress at Lowood and a close friend of Jane.
l ☐ They had an infectious disease.

3 Newspaper headlines • Number the newspaper headlines with the chapter in the story in which these events happen.

a ☐ **Ex-governess sees success at new village school**
b ☐ **Report into terrible conditions at school**
c ☐ **The Rochester Estate in ruins**
d ☐ Bigamist! Man hides his wife in attic for years

4 Themes • Match the sentences to their main theme. In which parts of the story do you find these themes? Who are the sentences about?

a Marriage
b The supernatural
c Education
d Social class
e Unhappiness and cruelty
f Money and independence

1. ☐ 'I was too poor and unimportant.'
2. ☐ 'Her uncle wanted to find her a good match…'
3. ☐ 'But things have changed. I am a rich woman now.'
4. ☐ 'I was aware that I had no money.'
5. ☐ '… she was also his wife. I knew that I could not marry him.'
6. ☐ 'They seemed to be very strict and unfriendly.'
7. ☐ 'I thought I saw shadows near the bed.'
8. ☐ 'He liked to frighten me and he made me very unhappy.'
9. ☐ 'Mr Rochester wants you to teach her in English.'
10. ☐ 'Take her to the red room and lock the door'.
11. ☐ 'I thought I heard a voice.'
12. ☐ '"You are his governess," she reminded me.'

5 Writing • Write a new ending. It does not have to be a fairy tale ending! What would make the characters happy or sad? You can take the viewpoint of a different character or tell the story as the narrator.

VALUES & FEELINGS

THE CHARACTERS

1 Use the words in the box to describe the characters. Make nouns from the adjectives for exercise 2.

cruel • courageous •
loving • loyal •
forgiving • dishonest •
impatient •
hardworking •
strong •
independent •
lonely • generous •
compassionate •
romantic • friendly •
proud

THINK!

2 Which values and feelings do you think each chapter is about? Choose one or more items from the box in exercise 1 and complete the table.

Chapters 1-3			
Chapters 4-6			
Chapters 7-9			

THE STORY

3 In the word cloud you can see a list of values and feelings: which ones can you associate with *Jane Eyre*? Justify your answers and write them in the box, dividing them into 'positive' and 'negative'.

> compassion generosity
> boredom friendship
> trust
> hope unhappiness anger
> patient freedom gratitude
> regret love suffering
> hurt
> forgiveness passion fear

POSITIVE	NEGATIVE
....	....
....	....
....	....
....	....

 YOUR TURN!

4 What about you? Now prepare your own word cloud using the words above. Make them big or small according to the importance they have for you.

This reader uses the expansive reading approach: where reading is not only the enjoyment of the story and the discovery of a new language, but an opportunity to make cultural connections.

The new language introduced in this step of our **Reading & Training Life Skills** series is listed below and language from lower steps is included too. For a complete list for all six steps, see *The Black Cat Graded Readers Handbook* at *blackcat-cideb.com*.

Step THREE B1.2

Verb tenses
Present Perfect Simple: unfinished past with *for* or *since* (duration form)
Past Perfect Simple: narrative

Verb forms and patterns
Regular verbs and all irregular verbs in current English
Causative: *have / get* + object + past participle
Reported questions and orders with *ask* and *tell*

Modal verbs
Would: hypothesis
Would rather: preference
Should (present and future reference): moral obligation
Ought to (present and future reference): moral obligation
Used to: past habits and states

Types of clause
2nd Conditional: *if* + past, *would(n't)*
Zero, 1st and 2nd conditionals with *unless*
Non-defining relative clauses with *who* and *where*
Clauses of result: *so; so ... that; such ... that*
Clauses of concession: *although, though*

Other
Comparison: *(not) as / so ... as; (not) ... enough to; too ... to*

Step Three
If you enjoyed this reader, try another one in Step Three...

- *Romeo and Juliet*, by William Shakespeare
- *Three Men in a Boat*, by J.K. Jerome **(Life Skills)**
- *The Importance of Being Earnest*, by Oscar Wilde

Step Four
...or take a step forward to Step Four!

- *Far from the Madding Crowd*, by Thomas Hardy
- *North and South*, by Elizabeth Gaskell **(Life Skills)**
- *Northanger Abbey*, by Jane Austen